Theology in Health ...tters

Edited by Hilary Dominic Regan

Theology in Health Care Matters

Catholic and Reformed Perspectives

Edited by Hilary Dominic Regan

Adelaide
2024

Agathon: A Journal of Ethics and Value in the Modern World
Volume 9, 2022

Agathon refers to the Greek word used by Plato in the Republic to refer to 'the good beyond being', most notably deployed in recent times by Iris Murdoch and Emmanuel Levinas, both of whom use this touchstone to situate ethics at the heart of all of philosophy

We live in an evolving and increasingly complex world but our ethical concepts have frequently struggled to keep pace with the change. As a result, much of what passes for public debate at present remains in the grip of either deterministic or consequentialist thinking, both built on outdated assumptions and both representing attempts to address major issues in the absence of ethical concepts. We suffer, as Iris Murdoch lamented, a 'loss of concepts, the loss of a moral and political vocabulary'.

The interdisciplinary journal, *Agathon*, seeks to bring together scholars from across the humanities, social sciences and sciences, including disciplines such as philosophy, theology, law and medicine, to engage with the ethical questions that now beset the modern world.

The journal is a home for considering questions such as how we deal with competing values in ethical discourse, how ethical theory finds expression in practice, what constitutes ethical character and how it is cultivated, and what excellence and wisdom look like for the ethical person or society in the twenty-first century.

Agathon is an international and interdisciplinary refereed journal published annually by ATF Press.

Chief Editor
Dr Paul Babie, University of Adelaide Law School Professor of the Theory and Law of Property

Editorial Board
- Professor Terence Lovat, Emeritus Professor, The University of Newcastle, Australia & Hon Fellow University of Oxford, UK.
- Professor Robert Crotty, former Director, Ethics Centre of South Australia, Emeritus Professor of Religion and Education, University of South Australia, Adelaide.
- Managing Editor and Publisher Mr Hilary Regan, Publisher, ATF Press Publishing Group, PO Box 234 Brompton, SA 5007, Australia. Email: hdregan@atf.org.au

Subscription Rates
Local: Individual Aus $55 Institutions Aus $65   Overseas: Individuals US $60 Institutions US $65

Agathon is published by ATF Press an imprint of the ATF Press Publishing Group which is owned by ATF (Australia) Ltd (ABN 90 116 359 963) and is published once a year. ISSN 2201-3563

ISBN: 978-1-923006-92-8   soft
         978-1-923006-93-5   hard
         978-1-923006-94-2   epub
         978-1-923006-95-9   pdf

SCAN ME

Published by:

An imprint of the ATF Press Publishing
Group owned by ATF (Australia) Ltd.
PO Box 234
Brompton, SA 5007
Australia
ABN 90 116 359 963
www.atfpress.com
Making a lasting impact

Agathon: A Journal of Ethics and Value in the Modern World, Vol 9/2022

Table of Contents

Agathon: A Journal of Ethics and Value in the Modern World, Vol 9/2022

Editorial

Health care is delivered in all parts of the world and in many different settings. In many countries health care is government sponsored and paid for. In some countries it also privately run either on a not-for-profit basis or for profit. Some large companies that run health care systems do so as one aspect of a diverse range of activities, or in other instances, as the sole activity that is undertaken. In many parts of the western world churches, Christian and non-Christian, are involved in health care delivery in hospitals, clinics and dispensaries. delivering medical, nursing and, at times, allied health facilities in urban and rural areas, in refugee camps and in areas of war or conflict.

Nurses, doctors and allied health professionals are trained locally or abroad to cater for an ever-increasing range of complex health care needs and situations. The COVID epidemic has raised new challenges for many places which are already over-stretched. In many parts of the world with longevity increasing there are new needs to be addressed and in other places an ever-increasing number of new-born children born into poverty raises a life time of needs to be addressed.

Over the last thirty years new medical agencies, sometimes linked to Church based aid and medical agencies, staffed by those who work as 'volunteers' on reduced salaries than what they would get 'back home', have been born to cater for people in diverse new 'crisis' situations. They cater for refugees, minorities, those who are the 'collateral' damage, those who are the innocent victims of war, and other emerging points of conflict. They care for those hit by artillery, bombs, mines, those who have become the human shields in war. They care for and heal, where possible, in situations surrounded by the stresses of war, disease and death for all the injured who are brought to them and all the victims of war inflicted injuries. Each day brings new casualties to their doors which often are in tents, or in mobile clinics, and bombed out shells that once were sophisticated medical facilities.

There are those who treat and deal with the consequences of war on both sides of any conflict. Both sides, in any conflict, have horrific injuries which need medical care.

At the same time there are companies who provide medical equipment and medical supplies all over the world. Drug companies are 'for profit' organisations who make profits in what they supply to the rich and the poor, and to all economies who need the supplies to provide the best care possible and prevent death for whatever reason.

In Europe, Asia, the Americas, Africa, Australia and the wider Pacific, a large number of people are employed to care for others in institutions which have been founded by organisations of the different Churches. Some of these institutions have been existence for hundreds of years. In many places new models of care provision by Church based agencies are emerging.

In many places around the world the Churches are also involved in educating a variety of health care and allied health care professionals in educational institutions.

This volume of essays aims to unpack theologically the issues behind what is undertaken in Christian based health care. Much has been written over the years on Christian ethics and health care. What is being addressed here is different. That is to say, the aim is to step back and to look at issues of what can be described as 'the God questions': what is the distinctive Christian character of these services, how do they differ to other health care systems, what is the identity which makes them unique at their deepest roots More than that, it is at another level to go even deeper to investigate the relationship between the Church and the world. For Church based institutions it is goes to 'God's self-revelation in Jesus Christ. He it is Who defines the nature of the Church and the world in their relationship and difference, since it is He Who is both the Creator Word and the Incarnate Word who reconciles the world to God; fulfils the divine purpose for creation', as Reformed theologian, Gordon Watson writes in this volume. Or as Catholic theologian Anthony Kelly when writes when referring to 'Catholic identity' in Church run institutions: 'Any talk of Catholic identity is, first of all, part of a much larger conversation; indeed, it contributes to the long conversation that the Church embodies, as it testifies to God's own Word becoming flesh in order to enter into the unending conversation we call 'human history'.

So, this volume of essays aims to examine to some theological issues in health care. It starts with former international leader of the Dominican Order, Timothy Radcliffe OP, examining and reflecting theologically on his own experience of being a patient in the National Health Service in the UK for major cancer surgery. He refers to his long hours of surgery, being cared for and recovery as being a time of learning 'a little more of what it means to live'. 'Sickness plunges us into the messy confusion of our bodily life, where God embraces us, even if with infinite discretion.'

The second article examines the work of a Director of Mission, Tony Brennan, in a Catholic hospital in Australia. He writes of his day: 'the role of a mission leader is to be open, to see, hear and act upon what the ever-present loving God is asking of us here and now. Profound formation and transformation is therefore a personal imperative within the role. Mission leaders do not work alone but collaborate in a community of practice which supports everyone in their community to deepen their understanding of what mission means for each and all.'

The third and fourth articles come from the Reformed theological tradition, written by systematic theologian Gordon Watson who taught in Brisbane for many years, and were written for a working party of the Uniting Church in Australia in Queensland in the 1990's where the Synod had asked a theological working group 'to report on the issue of the Church's involvement in the provision of Health Care'. The two articles are a solid investigation of the theological issues from a Reformed perspective.

The final two articles are from a Catholic perspective by well-known Catholic systematic theologian, Anthony Kelly CSsR. One article is on Catholic identity in institutions run by the Church and the other studies a vision of a Christian vision of a hospital. Of a Christian vision for a hospital, he writes: 'For the health professional there is a special a burden of looking into the face of suffering. Yes, there is hope, there is healing, and at the same time there is defeat, for a hospital is a laboratory of common humanity. We live, we die; and yet, even at that dark limit, Christian hope opens to life redeemed, restored, made whole in God.'

This volume has taken a considerably long time to put together. It is not the final or the only word on the topic. It represents only thoughts by two of the Christian traditions involved in health care in and has only male contributors. It was not possible to get a more comprehensive group of denominational or gender balance despite various attempts over several years. Despite these deficiencies, the hope is that it does raise questions, provoke thoughts, opens new doors of thinking to be pursued and challenges those who work in these institutions to look at a larger horizon, a bigger picture, behind what they do day in and day out as health care professionals so they can also say that 'theology in health care matters'.

Hilary Dominic Regan

Agathon: A Journal of Ethics and Value in the Modern World, Vol 9/2022

God in the Desert of Sickness[1]

Timothy Radcliffe OP

I celebrated Christmas 2022 with extra delight. Not just because I was and am still alive after major surgery but because I have learnt a little more of what it means to live. I hesitated to write about my illness. The sick can be self-centred; eyes glaze over as one recites the litany of one's pills and symptoms. Virginia Woolf tells the ill not to expect any sympathy. Those who are well need to get on with their own lives. I dare to do so because I hope it sheds a glimmer of light on our belief in our God who became incarnate.

I was admitted to hospital the day after the Assumption for an operation for cancer of the jaw. It took seventeen hours. I was out, bar a minute or two, for thirty hours. Five weeks in hospital were eventually followed by six weeks of radiotherapy. But on the Feast of the Immaculate Conception, I felt the first return of a hint of energy. There is still a long haul ahead but the corner has been turned. It is time to try to preach again.

This experience of illness was embraced by two great Marian feasts, which are both about Mary's body: the beginning of her life in the womb, and her sharing in Christ's victory over death. In the days after the operation, it was almost impossible to pray. I ran out of steam after the first words of the Our Father. Two prayers sustained me: the daily Eucharist livestreamed from Blackfriars, the gift of Christ's body, and the 'Hail Mary', whose few words embrace the all drama of bodily life, from the conception of her child, then one pregnant woman greeting another, and finally our prayers for help to live this present moment face its end, 'now and at the hour of our death.'

---

1. First published in *The Tablet* (London) 6 January 2023. Used with permission.

The trauma of this operation, with the removal of several inches of my jaw and its replacement with bone and tissue from my leg, opened a small window onto the Incarnation, the embodiment of divinity. Is so much religion boring because we have shoved God back into heaven, remote from dangerous intimacy?

Aquinas asserted that, 'I am not my soul'. If I stub my toe, it has no spiritual meaning, but surely every spiritual experience is bedded in our corporeality. Aquinas again: 'Nothing is in the mind that is not first in the senses.' Sickness plunges us into the messy confusion of our bodily life, where God embraces us, even if with infinite discretion.

Illness chipped away at the identity I had created and opened the door to a deeper one that was a gift to be discovered. Soon after I surfaced in the Blenheim Ward of the Churchill hospital in Oxford, UK, a young doctor sat by my bed and asked simple questions, including: 'Where are you?' I remembered the place was connected with Blenheim but it did not look like the Palace. I could not answer. I hoped that he would ask me who was the Prime Minister so that I could reply that I was not sure if Boris knew! Instead he asked me who was the monarch, the only question to which I gave the correct answer.

I was, he said, disorientated. The separation of the world of my dreams and of woken reality became porous. I read in the eyes of the nurses that I had been difficult. This time of confusion only lasted a couple of days, but it touched the heart of who I thought myself to be: a teacher and preacher, a writer for whom a certain clarity of mind was of the essence. The brief fragility of my hold on reality disclosed the profound unity of body, soul and spirit, whose dramas are interwoven. The Word became flesh and embraced us in our moments of clarity and confusion. He knows who we are even when we have lost our bearings and are engulfed in fog. I was blessed to discover that I was a brother of those who struggle with mental illness.

I have always loved to be up early, eager for the tasks of the day, but in those early weeks, I was deprived of all agency. I lay there, connected to myriad tubes, which pumped in a sugary drip twelve hours a day and carried away waste. I was constantly injected, tested, examined. Even when the tubes began to be removed, I could do nothing, not even wipe my own bottom. I worried endlessly whether anyone would get me a bedpan in time.

So my identity as an agent was also lost for a while. The nurses and doctors did their marvellous best, always asking my permission before any procedure. My fragile sense of self was nourished by their gaze and touch, their eyes and hands. We exist in the gaze others offer us.

This utter dependency was embraced by our God who became a helpless swaddled infant, incapable of anything, also needing his nose and his bottom to be wiped but held and beheld by his mother. He became the eyes and hands of God, gazing at edgy Nathaniel, at the argumentative Samaritan woman at the well, at the despised tax collector Matthew, and seeing God's friends and reaching out in touch to the sick. These nurses were ministers of the divine gaze and touch, as were my brethren who faithfully came and sat with me every day, even when I could not say anything.

Britain is a secular land, it is claimed, but the hospital was full of religion. A nurse showed me her favourite image of the Virgin. Another spotted my rosary and showed me hers. Others asked for prayers and promised them, whispering their allegiance to their God, Christian or Muslim. Most of them came from countries were religion is still part of the air they breathe. The National Health Service is said to be the religion of modern Britain, but it is a temple in which God is acknowledge and served every day.

A third challenge to my self-identity was in a sort of sensory deprivation. Like all of my family, I love my food and drink. I have always hesitated over Paul's words, 'For God's kingdom does not consist of food and drink' (Rom 14:17). Surely the word 'only' has dropped out. Taste is a fundamental to the openness of the body to what is other and so one's sense of self. But for weeks, I was 'nil by mouth'. I felt trapped within myself, and thought often of Hopkins' bitter lines: 'My taste was me.' When at last I could hobble around on a Zimmer frame, I loved to clean my hands with the sanitizer and smell the hint of alcohol.

I first woke with a raging thirst, which alternated with a panicky feeling that I was drowning in the liquid pouring down my throat. For weeks I was not permitted to drink anything, just to dampen my lips with a wet sponge. All I could think of was Israel's tormented desire for water as she wandered in the wilderness, not trusting in the Lord who brought forth water from the rock. I obsessively repeated the words from Psalm 81, 'By the waters of Meribah I tested you.' In this desert, one must trust in the Lord, for whom one thirsts. On feast days we sing those lovely words from Psalm 62.

O God, you are my God, for you I long,
For you my soul is thirsting.
My body pines for you
Like a dry weary land without water.

God became human to share our thirst and teach us how to live it well: a baby thirsting for his mother's milk, parched for forty days in the wilderness, asking the Samaritan woman at the well for a drink, and finally dehydrated on the cross.

In *Soif,* a novel by Amelie Notbomb, Jesus delights in thirst. 'Having panted with thirst for a while, don't drink the goblet of water straight down. Take a mouthful, keep it in your mouth before swallowing it. Measure how marvellous it is.' So once again, deprivation followed by new gift. 'Taste and see that the Lord is good.' (Ps 34:8). So often it was the words of psalms that shone the light. How marvellous was that first sip of water, the beauty of which I had never known before.

The Hail Mary ends with asking for Mary's prayers 'now and at the hour of our death.' A previous bout of cancer had awoken me to my mortality. Now death had called to tell me that it was on the way. My consultant told me the survival rate for this operation is sixty per cent after five years. Is that a long time or short? I am not sure. I might live for much longer or less, but surely the summons is to live now. There is no other preparation for eternal life. Who are the people whose forgiveness I must seek? Who are those whom I love but have never told them? What are the acts of kindness that I must do today? There is no time to lose.

Agathon: A Journal of Ethics and Value in the Modern World, Vol 9/2022

A Day in the Life of a Director of Mission

Tony Brennan

Abstract: Every day is different. Director of Mission at Calvary Health Care is a unique role—integral to the organisation's work but yet its mission can sometimes feel marginal in a busy private hospital. Pope Francis described the whole Christian church as a 'field hospital' on mission for the most vulnerable. Within this global field of care stands the role of a Director of Mission (DOM). The DOM role stands in a long tradition of similar roles, vocations and ministries within Christianity and Catholicity, both in the midst and at the edge of projects like social welfare, health care and education. The role of a mission leader is to be open, to see, hear and act upon what the ever-present loving God is asking of us here and now. Profound formation and transformation is therefore a personal imperative within the role. Mission leaders do not work alone but collaborate in a community of practice which supports everyone in their community to deepen their understanding of what mission means for each and all. 'Mission' is a word with deep sources in Christian scripture and history which has been used at the vanguard of efforts to spread the good news of the life and teachings of Jesus. 'Mission' was a word Mary Potter used; in the late nineteenth century she founded a breakaway movement of religious women dedicated to go to the margins of society when church and state frowned on her sisters leaving the silent cloister. With the support of the Pope she initiated the first Catholic hospital in Rome and in so doing began the mission of the Little Company of Mary that is Calvary's foundation charism. Active contemplative spirituality finds expression today in Catholic social and bioethical teachings. Calvary since its governance origins in 2013 has developed a Mission Framework drawn from these foundational teachings and sources. Tony Brennan (Director of Mission—Calvary Health Care Hobart) reflects on these themes, sources and challenges through the lens of an ordinary day. A day which calls him to provide pastoral care for a grieving family, confront workplace racism and respond to a contemporary ethical dilemma. An ordinary day but containing extraordinary 'mission' calls.

Tony Brennan has been Director of Mission at Calvary Health Care Hobart for four years. Prior to that worked for the Society of St Vincent de Paul for four years and in Catholic Education for twenty five. He has a Masters in Educational Leadership and a Masters of Theology. Married to Kate, he has three adult children and enjoys writing songs and poetry and bushwalking in Tasmania.

> *8:00am, 18/03/2021 I arrived Calvary St John's. I hand sanitise and have my temperature checked at the COVID-19 Screening station. Soon I've landed at a hot-desk and I am checking through the overnight email. I notice a few things of interest floating up amongst the normal flotsam and jetsam: I'm delighted to read that the National CEO has announced a Reconciliation Action Plan working party; I flag an email from a staff member who is asking a challenging bioethical question; and I note my reminder alarm that the Pastoral Care Team is on retreat off-site so I will be on-call holding the Pastoral Care pager.*

There are no ordinary days and no two days of a Director of Mission are the same. However, checking emails can be the very ordinary start to many extraordinary days. I send to our Volunteer Services Manager some quick replies and proofread her newsletter which has kept 120 volunteers connected during the pandemic year—she shares her progress in restoring these volunteers to their old or new Covid-safe roles after a year stood down. As Director of Mission I very rarely need to back-fill for our high performing Calvary Hobart Pastoral Care Team. Today they are gathering at a retreat centre in the ferny foothills of Mt Wellington also known by its *palawa kani* name *Kunanyi*. Knowing the work the skilled pastoral care practitioners do year round to accompany patients and fellow staff with the stress and grief of life and the journey of healing, I have some trepidation whether the Pastoral Care pager in my pocket will go off today and what moments I will be called into in their stead. However, Calvary Hobart needs its Pastoral Care Team members to have this retreat day, so that they may to reflect on the inspiration that nourishes them in their own spiritual and personal mission and journey, in order that they can be resilient in their care for others. Likewise my role requires me to have opportunities for spiritual and personal formation in order that I remain connected to the focus and inspiration of the Calvary Mission, a God that transforms human experience, calls us out of self-absorption into a mission of presence with others, and in particular those who are most marginalised and vulnerable. Ultimately 'God is essentially missionary'[1] and the 'mission' is God's, not ours. We've been simply recruited like hopefully willing volunteers.

> *8:30am, I meet with the Clinical Services Manager at St John's—a sub-acute hospital half the size of our Lenah Valley Hospital with efficient theatres and a palliative care ward, and I ask him my habitual question "how's your hospital". As happens every couple of weeks I present him with a pack of certificates, each with paper-clipped coffee vouchers. He will hand these out in meetings with Unit Managers and on rounding. Each certificate includes the verbatim gratitude of patients for named staff directly copied from survey feedback—there is no clearer reinforcement of our collective mission of 'being for others' than these messages of gratitude in the patient's own words..*

How is a Catholic hospital and all those who work in it to understand what 'mission' is twenty centuries after the founding of the church? The wards of Calvary no longer witness the purposeful pace of white dressed and blue veiled Sisters of the Little Company of Mary. The culture of the Roman Catholic Church will never again feel as all-pervasive as eighty years ago when the Archbishop of Hobart opened Calvary Hospital in Lenah Valley. Nonetheless our Catholic hospital would not exist if not for an historic and universal call. Perhaps the best characterisation of this tradition and the church's expectation of Catholic hospitals is Pope Francis' own description of the church as 'a field hospital that takes in the weakest people: the infirm'.[2] The Greek word for church is *ecclesia*, which means an assembly who are literally 'called out'. 'Mission' (Latin: *missionem*) means the 'act of sending' and in Jesus' commissioning of the disciples (Mt 28:16–20; Luke 24: 44–49) there is an unequivocal universal sending of Christ's disciples to all nations and all peoples.

---

1. Noel Connolly, 'Mission: Mother of the Church and of Theology', Compass: a Review of Topical Theology, 40/1 (2006): 4–5.
2. Devin Watkins, (2019, August 28). 'Pope at Audience: Church a "field hospital" that cares for sick' retrieved 12 April 2021 from Vatican News: https://www.vaticannews.va/en/pope/news/2019-08/pope-francis-general-audience-church-cares-for-sick.html.

The Mission is God's and we in the church are called to go forth into it (*Evangelli Gaudium, 2013,* §20). Nonetheless in contemporary missiology there are competing ecclesiologies that uphold or protest the centrality of the church in God's plan.[3] There are those who emphasise 'Catholic Identity' and an inward looking Church that seeks new membership but Pope Francis puts a different view:

> The church is called to come out of herself and to go to the peripheries . . . When the church does not come out of herself to evangelize, she becomes self-referential and then gets sick.[4]

This outward mission is what Mary Potter, the foundress of the Little Company of Mary, intended and expressed in direct 'sending' of sisters to Australia one hundred and thirty-five years ago, with the hope of providing care for the most vulnerable. Pope Francis defines church as 'those who are called out' and wants a church 'which is poor for the poor' and 'evangelised by them' (§198). A program of evangelization cannot lose sight that its foundational sense is 'good news for the poor' (Lk 4:18) and thereby moves from a narrow definition of proclamation to a 'pastoral response'[5]. It is this sense that the Calvary mission, within this broader theological and historical mission is always directed towards the margins, just as the first actions of the Little Company of Mary in Nottingham and in Sydney was to set up soup kitchens for the poor.

One might ask 'how is a private hospital serving the margins?' How is a Catholic private hospital and all those who work in it to understand what 'mission' calls for when the majority of their patient intake has the means to pay for private health insurance or opt for elective surgery? One important answer is that Australians of all degrees of advantage engage with private as well as public hospitals, given the Australian health care system's complex integration. This

---

3. Jim D'Orsa & Therese D'Orsa, *Leading for Mission* (Mulgrave: Vaughan Publishing, 2013), 7–8.

4. Thomas C Fox, (2013, March 27). Francis pre-conclave remarks echo in first general audience. Retrieved April 6, 2021, from National Catholic Reporter: http://ncronline.org/blogs/ncr-today/francis-pre-conclave-remarks-echo-first-general-audience.

5. Philip Malone, 'From Gaudium et Spes to Evangelii Gaudium: from Proclamation to Pastoral Response', in Compass: a Review of Topical Theology, 50 (Autumn, 2016): 3–5.

hospital was effectively commandeered by the Federal Government for several months last year due to the COVID-19 pandemic as were all private hospitals. Calvary Hobart as a private hospital also welcomes patients on public waiting lists as negotiated with the state health service in managing their waiting lists. However, the question is an important one, given the clearest touchstone of mission integrity in church agencies would be as Pope Francis commends us to go to the peripheries. The Little Company of Mary Sisters as they arrived in Sydney in 1885 and Hobart in 1938 had few resources and appealed to the largess of wealthy benefactors and the generous donations of the local Catholic community.

In the decades following two depressions, Catholics as a population cohort were themselves most often at the margins economically and culturally. Today, Calvary is a not-for-profit health care group and asserts this in this in the positive as well; that it is a for-purpose health care service. That purpose includes quality clinical care and successful business operations but its 'purpose' most essentially is to fulfil its mission. Today, the mission to go the margins remains the imperative but, amidst the complex business and clinical operation of private health care the mission, to make the vulnerable more welcome, can appear marginal to core business. Calvary Tasmania has made significant contributions to the local community over twenty years through its Community Grants ($50000 per annum). Furthermore its Mary Potter Foundation has partnered with doctors to care for patients suffering financial hardship. In 2020 several families on Working Visas and therefore without Medicare were thus assisted to have their baby at Calvary given they would have been charged the full cost in the public health system.

9:00am, as the St John's Café opens, I play guitar in the hall while enjoying a coffee, and count how many staff, patients and visitors smile with the gentle therapy of music. On one occasion a family stopped and listen then invited me to play in their mother's room while she was in the last stages of dying. I move down to the Gibson palliative care ward and the chemotherapy lounge to do the same. Playing there recently I witnessed the Gibson palliative care nurses, admin staff and housekeepers all gather as is their renewed tradition to make a moment's guard of honour as funeral directors remove the body of a patient who has died. Imagine the privilege of being a musician: I moved to put down my guitar but was asked to keep playing.

Mary Potter (b London, 1847—d Rome, 1913) founded the Sisters of the Little Company of Mary in 1877 in a disused stocking factory in central England town of Nottingham, but soon suffered the censure of her local bishop. Preferring pious women to be reserved in the cloister and resistant to Potter's theology which revered the experience or religious women[6], Bishop Bagshawe did not agree with her active and contemplative mission nor her particular inspiration for the sisters to be in constant prayer and service for the dying.[7] Calvary Health Care takes its name from this core image of women praying at the foot of the cross—*Calvaria* is Latin for 'a bare skull' and the translation of *Golgotha*, 'the place of the skull' outside the walls of Jerusalem where the crucifixion of Jesus of Nazareth took place in c 29 CE. Today the name's Christian origin and confronting imagery may come as a shock to the 1,000 clinical and corporate staff

in Hobart. Mary Potter went to Rome in 1882 partly to allow the spread of the Little Company of Mary's mission to be unrestrained by local ecclesial restrictions. There she oversaw a mother house planned in a cruciform with a heart shaped chapel under its central dome. It contained a hospice and Rome's first Catholic hospital. The daily footsteps of every sister travelling between the convent and the hospice, were on a well-trodden path past the Blessed Sacrament and the altar. To express her mission she had a triptych painted to depict this active-contemplative spirituality: under the crucifixion scene are the images of a Little Company Sister kneeling in prayer and beside it two sisters caring for a patient at the bedside [Figure 1]. One hundred and

Figure 1

6.   Elizabeth West, *One Woman's Journey: Mary Potter—Founder Little Company of Mary* (Spectrum publications: Richmond, Vic, 2000), 81.

7.   Patrick Dougherty, *Mother Mary Potter- Foundress of Little Company of Mary* (Sands and Co, London, 1961) 127.

eleven years after the founding of her order, which had since spread throughout the world, Pope John Paul II declared Mother Mary Potter 'Venerable'.

> *10:30am, I have finished up at St John's in South Hobart and driven 20 minutes across Hobart to Lenah Valley for two morning calendar appointments, firstly a Consultative Committee meeting between Executive members, union reps and staff representing corporate areas (which include Hospitality, admin staff and allied health teams (including physiotherapists) discussing work hours issues; and secondly a presentation to a group of Hospitality staff about bullying and racist harassment.*

In contemporary healthcare real workplace issues arise regularly about the nature and challenges of their clinical and non-clinical roles, and the question of cultural safety regarding race and ethnicity has also arisen. I worked recently with the Hospitality Services Manager who noticed racist comments being made among her 120 kitchen and housekeeping staff. Human Resources staff based at Regional Office advised the best response was an education campaign with session, which we titled 'Don't be a silent witness' to encourage a change in the culture, to support new staff and allow a ventilation of fears and anxieties of older staff. I have always been fascinated with what motivates people to act or instead to be bystanders when there are temptations to exclude others in their workplaces and in culture generally.[8]

In my own formation, working in social welfare for five years and education for twenty-five and now health care for four years, all in the Catholic sector, the inspiration of my life has been men and women like Mary Potter who felt a mission to struggle for a better world in which all people, regardless of gender, race, wealth or other differences were all of equal dignity before God, given that 'there is neither Jew nor Greek, woman or man for you are one in Christ Jesus' (Gal 3:28). Born in 1965 at the conclusion of the Second Vatican Council its reforming documents such as *Lumen Gentium* and *Gaudium et Spes* have been foundational and a formative 'call to action' for me. I found

---

8. Catherine C Sanderson, *Why We Act: Turning Bystanders into Moral Rebels* (Belknap Press of Harvard University Press: Cambridge Massachusetts, 2000), 206.

a missionary call echoed in the Church's teachings at the highest levels which called from Potter's own times for the local church to attend to the needs of the most marginalised, and this call has been continued to Pope Francis in the present day. Leaders in this mission were called to discern 'the signs of the times', to move away from a narrow adherence to legalistic deductive reasoning but to acknowledge lived experience and to give primacy to love understood richly as pastoral compassion modelled by Jesus in the Gospels.[9]

> *Noon, at the coffee shop we call the Little Company Café, I witness an encounter between a tired part-time theatre nurse clothed in scrubs and a just arrived neurosurgeon in his tailored suit. As I wait nearby in the queue, the nurse with a cheeky smile teased the surgeon, given that all doctors receive free coffee, that she would happily receive now the coffee he had promised to buy her a year ago. He agreed with some chagrin. In that the surgeon seemed in a better mood, she pressed her luck saying 'mind you, if I was to buy you a coffee on behalf of all the theatre nurse and assistants, you'd never drink a better coffee in your life'.*

Please forgive this daydream that came to me as I stood in the coffee queue and reimagined a scene from the Gospel (Jn 4). Nonetheless I am convinced that Christ continues his mission among us today and calls us into his presence in every day phenomena of email and café queues. It's true that the Gospel accounts have been distorted far worse than my effort here and applied even by Christians to justify terrible injustices such as slavery, sexism and anti-Semitism. Even the word 'mission' can jar First Nations people with their own generational trauma associated with the word. Yet remarkably through twenty centuries the core prophetic elements of Christianity seem to have subverted global systems which would otherwise prefer to champion the powerful at the expense of the powerless.[10] Perhaps it's my formation but I cannot read the Gospels (for example Matt 25:39–46) without seeing the clear through-line to Catholic Social Teaching including the dignity of the human person, the preferential option for the poor

---

9.   Peter J Henriot, Edward P DeBerri, Michael J Schultheis, *Catholic Social Teaching: Our Best Kept Secret* (Orbis Books: Maryknoll, New York, 1988), 18–19.
10. Tom Holland, *Dominion: the Making of the Western Mind* (Little Brown: London, 2019), 525.

and the interrelationship of love and justice.[11] Today Calvary Health Care has articulated organisational values which are ever-present mission summaries for staff: hospitality, respect, healing and stewardship are likewise founded in social principles like the promotion of the common good, solidarity of all peoples and stewardship of the natural world, which Pope Francis has called Our Common Home (Laudate Si, 2015). Less well known by all Calvary staff but instrumental for Directors of Mission like myself, and becoming increasingly significant for leaders of all levels, from wards to the Board, is the Mission Governance Framework [Figure 2]. These ten mission focus areas are direct reporting elements (expressed as key performance indicators to concur with the lexicons and processes of modern corporate life) and it is

Figure 2: Mission Governance Framework elements and focus *areas*

an easy matching exercise to draw their connections directly to the principles at the core of Catholic Social teaching. By the way the Mission Accountability Framework, as it was first titled in 2016 and revised as the Mission Governance Framework in 2020, has immediately been

---

11. Henriot *et al, Catholic Social Teaching,* 20–22.

given great importance at the highest levels of Calvary governance, at the National Executive Team, the Little Company of Mary Board which it reports to and ultimately Calvary Ministries which continues the determined independent governance—the legacy of Potter's struggles with parochial church leaders.

> *1:00pm, the Pastoral Care pager buzzes loudly and I almost spill my coffee. 'On call', given that the Pastoral Care Team are on their annual retreat day, I read on the pager that our Critical Care Unit have sought urgent Pastoral Care support. Reporting immediately to the ward, I meet the duty nurse in charge sitting with a man who is weeping. His wife of forty years was fit and well three weeks ago as they holidayed in Tassie, felt unwell over the weekend and was brought into Accident and Emergency. After a series of heart attacks she is now critically ill on a respirator with a poor prognosis. I introduce myself and for the next few hours accompany them in a series of meetings with emergency and critical care doctors. I am in awe of the way the Duty Nurse and the CCU Nurse Unit Manager dignify the father and his two adult sons. Every question is answered gently and honestly. We get the family sandwiches and coffees and lead them to a meeting room where they can have some privacy. In a few moments away from the family I email Mark Green, National Director of Mission, to apologise for late notice absence from the national teleconference.*

As I sit with the family there are two thoughts which I reflect upon: firstly the extraordinary daily work of Pastoral Care and secondly the extraordinary contemplative and active support of the National Mission Group led by Mark Green. It is a profound privilege to sit with those who are dying and those who love them. Likewise I have had the experience in the past to sit with a family member as the Critical Care Unit nurses wash the body of the one who has died, referring to them by name at all times: ('now Dan, we're just going to roll you over').

Pastoral Care is a central role in the mission and purpose of a Catholic hospital:[12] Accompanying vulnerable people in these

---

12. Maryanne Confoy, *Welcome, Inclusion, Attentive Presence: the Central role of Pastoral Care in Catholic Health and Aged Care* (Catholic Health Australia: Red Hill, ACT, 2015), 5.

intense moments of grief, fear and anxiety is profoundly confronting and humbling. I see in the work of our Pastoral Care practitioners a radical attention to the journey of the other that dignifies the patient—the sick, the dying, the dead and those who love them. Nonetheless as I sit with the family, I am embarrassed to admit my mind drifts to the National Mission meeting that I regret missing. Calvary Mission leaders are not solo acts but collaborate in a gifted team of mission practice which supports everyone in their local work to deepen their understanding of what mission means for each and all. It is an incredible support to me in my role to have a weekly teleconference with our team of a dozen Directors of Mission and Mission Integration Officers. Our National Director of Mission, sets the tone and culture of these meetings which allow significant time for reflection and prayer—sometimes half the meeting, along with occasional times of formation where the whole time is allocated to the purpose of spiritual support for each of us on the journey. Mark prepares a detailed agenda and there are always pressing matters for quick decisions and more substantive matters flagged for some dedicated time when available. The meetings have a spirit of joy though sometimes we come together with weariness or worry. An extraordinary list of actions has arisen from these meetings with each of the team stepping forward in some area of attention or expertise and also taking turns to lead the reflection. In addition Mark schedules monthly one-to-one catch-ups with all of us so that we can raise questions or seek wise counsel on diverse matters—nothing in our role is off the agenda. The work of a Director of Mission often feels singular operationally but is in fact highly collaborative and mutually supporting. I place a candle on the table as I sit with the family, and I feel that the support and prayers of the National Mission leaders are with us also.

A bit after 2:00 pm, I meet with a staff member from Patient Admin. Her email had asked whether I run a committee which makes decisions about whether a patient should receive surgery at Calvary. I guessed the unstated issue was regarding gender-reassignment after several recent requests for admission that had been noted by our administration staff as having conflicting gender information on a simple patient ID check.

Here was a staff member whose moral compass was spinning, perplexed—even scandalised[13]—that she may be put in a future moral dilemma simply by exercising her normal work duties. Her experience was that her Patient Administration co-workers had noticed that a patient's request for a surgical procedure had a different gender recorded on the surgeon's admission request compared with what was listed in the medical records. As I listened it impressed me to witness a staff member acting on their sense of conscience with moral courage.[14] I had already begun composing an email to brief my colleagues and the national DOM group about my actions in regard to the same dilemma, which had emerged in the weeks prior. I had consulted the Catholic Health Australia (CHA) Code of Ethical Standards[15] (specifically section 3:11), approached Mark Green who in turn approached respected ethicist Bernadette Tobin of the Plunkett Centre at Australian Catholic University. I was asked by the Hobart Director of Clinical Services to contact the surgeon and did so explaining Calvary's perspective that we had no information about the wellbeing of the patient, the purpose of the surgery (double mastectomy) or whether the intervention was directly therapeutic for a pathological condition. The surgeon was able to confirm there was no therapeutic or preventative basis for the removal of healthy tissue. Based on the above advice I communicated that the procedure was not one undertaken at a Catholic Hospital without such grounds and the surgeon was satisfied with this and removed the request for admission.

> *3:30 pm, I head to North Hobart for an off-site working party of our Consumer Advisory Group (CAG). This meeting with two staff and two volunteer consumer representatives also includes two invitees of ethnic communities, the Indian and Nepalese communities, which are two prominent groups interacting with the hospital. Our meeting comes up with messaging to present to staff to help them comprehend the miss-communications that can affect their community members.*

---

13. *Catholic Health Australia, Code of Ethical Standards for Catholic Health and Aged Care Services in Australia* (Catholic Health Australia: Red Hill, ACT, 2001), 65.
14. Dr Dan Fleming, 'Conscience at the heart organisation' in Catholic Health Australia, Code of Ethical Standards for Catholic Health and Aged Care Services in Australia, Supplementary Papers (Catholic Health Australia: Red Hill, ACT, 2016), 71.
15. Catholic Health Australia, 2001 30.

Another part of my Director of Mission role is to lead our hospital wide response to the Partnering with Consumers Standard of the National Safety and Quality Health Standard.[16] Even if this Standard did not exist, it would surely be my role to invent it based on our Mission Governance priority of Person Centred Care. There are fourteen sub-elements of the NSQHS Standard all of which in some respect are requiring modern Australian health care institutions to truly partner with their patients and their loved ones—to ensure their voice is heard and that their clinical healing is not just something done to them but with which they participate actively and with their dignity safeguarded. Another function of the Standard is to ensure active ongoing and authentic consultation of consumer representatives, thus the Consumer Advisory Group and CAG Working Party. Along with the positive patient feedback to staff that we return to them via a certificate signed by the General Manager, every critical piece of feedback or complaint is followed up rigorously, providing insight of experience that we can improve for other patients. Reconciliation with First Nations peoples has been an issue that has captured my attention since high school given the appalling history of their dispossession in Tasmania.[17] If these most vulnerable people such as aboriginal Australians and those from culturally and linguistically diverse communities are made to feel welcome at our hospitals, it underlines our Calvary maxim that 'all are welcome'.

> *5:00 pm, I drive out but I am anticipating I might get a call from the Regional CEO. The car phone rings and I answer (hands free). The complexity she has oversite of in Victoria and Tasmania is extraordinary, made more difficult by the pandemic year. When the call finishes I still have a few moments to reflect as I always do on the day, and to ask myself what three moments am I most grateful for or feel most honoured to have experienced?*

Our National CEO Martin Bowles led the installation of a Regional Structure in 2019 to install support structures which would support local Calvary hospitals, community care services and aged

16. Australian Commission on Safety and Quality in Health Care, https://www. safetyandquality.gov.au/standards/nsqhs-standards, retrieved 21 April 2021.
17. Henry Reynolds, *Why Weren't We Told? Personal search for the truth about our history* (Ringwood, Vic.: Penguin, 2000).

care facilities to be ready for the decade ahead, which promises extraordinary technological and demographic changes for Calvary Health Care. I was delighted recently when our Regional CEO, Cynthia Dowell brought together key leaders from Victoria and northern and southern Tasmania to envisage this future and the steps to take towards it. In contrast, Cynthia is calling me to check in on the Tasmanian Calvary Community Council that continues the benevolent grants the Little Company of Mary Sisters initiated it in 2002. So, here in this conversation, as I note it so often in my day, is the convergence of the stories of an inspiring heritage of compassion with the new stories of aspiration to continue this tradition of compassionate care in innovative ways that the Sisters in the blue veils could never have anticipated. The call is a brief check-in and as I turn the corner towards home, I ask myself what three moments I want to recollect and celebrate from this day, the 18th of March, 2021. Sitting in prolonged stillness and silence with the grieving father and his sons was profound, and reminded me of the unique ministry of Pastoral Care practitioners in accompanying those who grieve and mourn and the healing mystery of compassion. Secondly I remember the conversation between consumer representatives and ethnic community members that reminded me how frightening our hospital must feel for culturally and linguistically diverse people. The third moment that underlined the ordinary and extraordinary of my role was that afternoon conversation with the admin staffer in which she felt safe to query the ethics of her organisation's processes in regard to vulnerable members of the LGBTIQ community. As I head up Davey Street I mutter a prayer I've taught myself:

> *I pray for all creation and all creatures, for all people in all places and for those I love and all those they love.*
> *I pray for the poor and those who help them, for the sick and those serve them.*
> *I pray for the dying and those who tend them, for the dead and those who mourn them.*
> *I pray that I may love myself and the hard to love. I pray for a good life and a good death.*
> *I pray that I may more mirror Godself in this life and the next.*

Agathon: A Journal of Ethics and Value in the Modern World, Vol 9/2022

Some Issues Related to the Hospital Task Group's Expectations of 'Theological Input'

Gordon Watson

A discussion paper for the 'theological task group' of the Synod Hospitals Task Group for the Uniting Church in Australia, Queensland Synod, by The Rev Dr Gordon Watson

The problem before the task group is one of deciphering the nature of ethical/theological meaning in the relationship between 'the church' in its institutional form as Synod and its relationships with institutional forms of its mission, viz, hospitals.

Stanley Hauerwas, one of the most provocative contemporary Christian writers on ethics, notes in his book, *Vision and Virtue: Essays in Christian Ethical Reflection* Notre Dame. 1974, that contemporary ethical analysis concentrates on problems; situations in which it is hard to know what to do. In such a situation ethics is understood as a procedure for making decisions, for resolving conflict of choice situations. This model of ethics assumes that no one faces an ethical issue until they find themselves in a quandary: should I or should I not have an abortion for example. The moral life appears concerned primarily with hard decisions.

This picture of ethics is not accidental according to Hauerwas for the assumption that most of our moral concerns are 'problems' suggests that ethics can be construed as a rational science that evaluates alternative solutions. Moral decisions can then be seen to be resolvable on the basis of rationally derived principles that are not directly related to any particular set of moral convictions.

Ethics in this case can then be understood as a branch of decision theory and can be taught as a disinterested social science. Hauerwas's criticism of current ethical theory aims at the influence of the Kantian ideal of rationally derived principles which are universally applicable.

The problems associated with this standard account of moral reasoning are largely unnoticed because we have become conditioned by the tacit presuppositions of our culture that the individual rational self is that which endows the world of public facts with meaning.

Thus from the perspective of the standard account, which is the object of Hauerwas's critique, such things as beliefs, dispositions and above all character cannot be the subject of rational analysis and are therefore seen as irrelevant to ethical discourse. They are subjective variants which need to be isolated from the process of ethical decision making. It would seem that one only needs to state the implications of the standard account of ethical reasoning to see that it is inadequate from the perspective of Christian ethics.

We cannot account for moral decision making solely in terms of the rationality of the decision making process. We need to take into account those factors which form us as the people we are. It is these tacit factors which make up who we are which will determine what kind of moral considerations we will regard as rational and consequently to which we will give weight in our moral decision making.

> For example, the language that we use to describe our behaviour to ourselves and others is not uniquely ours. We share a common cultural and social context which makes it possible for us to communicate with each other. So what makes it possible for us to check the truthfulness of ours and others account of their moral behaviour is the personal relationships and the social context in which our moral ideas gain their credibility. We cannot in other words make our behaviour mean anything we want, even what we may think is the most reasonable action must make sense not only to us but must be congruent with the assumptions and beliefs embedded in the language which we use.

If Christianity is to be self consistent it must take Jesus Christ as the human expression of God's reality and truth. This seeming imperialist claim on the part of Christianity is simply a way of giving expression to the fact that in any particular culture what is most real, what is important will be defined by the dominant world view. It may not be the view of the majority of the inhabitants of any given society but it will be the view which gives meaning to the public culture and the issues of the public agenda which are seen to be important. It will articulate a world view that absorbs the world.

The world which we inhabit, that is the culture of the society in which we live, is one which is pervasively influenced by the 'modern' world view, this is a view of reality which derives from the Enlightenment. Reality is that which can be defined by our measurement of it. The material world can be described accurately by us in terms of models which are basically mechanical and mathematical. The reality of the other person is less real than our own mind and thought. From this disembodied position everything else whether persons or things are useable and or discardable. As Colin Gunton pointed out in his book *The One, The Three and the Many* (Cambridge, 1993, 12), 'modernity is characterised by a philosophy of non-relation, of disengagement, in which human subjects standing apart from each other and the world use each other and the world as instruments'.

The modern penchant for the economic philosophy called 'monetarism' or economic rationalism, as the panacea of all social and economic questions is the old idea of Adam Smith's 'hidden hand' of market forces in modern dress. It assumes that we do not belong to God and each other but are our own; this entails that others are there for whatever purposes happen to be marketable.

The dominant view of our culture is that *'we'* are the world: we absorb the world and give it meaning at the expense of community and the natural environment. Post modernism in its critique of modernity came to prominence as a consequence of its recognition that the world as it is in itself, the world apart from our description of it, is inaccessible to human beings. Thus the schools of post modernity view language as to all intents and purposes the only reality; the attempt is made to shift attention from study of the world as an objective entity to the study of texts and the various cultural linguistic realities which make up the world. The world *is* not *the* world but a multitude of small textual worlds; the linguistic worlds in which we live and move and have our being. Thus there is no such thing as the truth. There is merely this truth or that truth according to the operating context; there is my truth and your truth. All we have recourse to is a shifting sea of relativities none of whose views can be compared critically.

The problem with such views as purveyed by some post-modern critics of modernity is that just such claims as they make presuppose the very God's eye view of which they are so critical and which they intend their account of language to refute. It is a classic example of the famous Cretin saying, 'all Cretins are liars'.

Despite their seemingly opposite views of reality the modern and post modern world views share the notion that human reason can be the final arbiter of what is real or true. In place of the Enlightenment or modern view that what I see is what is there, that reason is a window onto a universal state of affairs, the post-modern view is that 'my facts' are 'my facts' and 'your facts' are 'your facts'; the world of post modernism consists of many worlds, many contexts, many truths.

Whilst post modernism offers valuable criticism of the dogmatism of reason based on the Enlightenment view of the world it too is subject to the same danger of the dogmatism of reason. Relativism and its colleague, political correctness, now replaces the old fashion idea of factual correctness. The problem with the culture of post modernity is that whereas in modern culture it was assumed that there could be dispute about the facts of the case and a sense of the commonality of the language used to describe the facts, now whole groups of people regard themselves as immune from criticism and at the same time treat other groups of people as tools or objects to be stereotyped, or in other ways minimised or ridiculed. To some feminists all men are rapists and men are not allowed to object to this label; some ethnic groups label all members of what is perceived as the dominant racial group as oppressors and exploiters who cannot do or say anything to exonerate themselves. Prejudice, intolerance and abuse may not be new phenomena associated with human relationships but post modernism insulates such behaviour from any criticism. As Colin Gunton has astutely observed some of the more strident examples of post modern criticism amount to no more than corporate or group veneer on the presuppositions of modernity.

Now in terms of the claims of Christian ethics it is important to see, in the context of a culture in which the predominant views are alien to its presuppositions, that human life has a characteristic unity and purpose in a context which establishes who we are as persons in relationship to God and each other. This unity is not a creation of the human mind or an arbitrary choice of some group interest but derives from the nature of Christ and the Spirit as God's personal presence with and for the creature in creation and reconciliation and promised redemption. By this personal presence of Christ and the Spirit there is established in history a context in which a narrative or story of human personhood becomes the truth of human relationships to God and each other. The answer to the question, 'What am I to do'? is 'I am to do what I am become'. We are to act in accordance with what it has *been given to me to be* as a member of the Body of Christ.

The question as I see it for this 'theological task group' is to spell out what this may mean for the church's commitment to the health care of the community of which it is a part by its provision of hospitals.

To examine how one would go about asking what such a commitment may entail I take as an illustration R Neibuhr's program of ethical decision making. Here the problem of relating ethical questions to institutions, such as churches and hospitals, is not seen as a variants of the question, 'What am I to do'? 'I am to do what I am become.' Act in accordance with what it has *been given to me to be* as a member of the Body of Christ. The ethical question here has to do with the more abstract idea of 'justice.' But the universal influence of the Niebuhrian ethical paradigm in Anglo/American culture led to the rather disturbing conclusion drawn by James Gustafson in which he is saying that ethics understood via the Niebuhrian paradigm makes Christianity unintelligible to itself.

James Gustafson in 1978 wrote an article titled, 'Theology confronts technology in the life sciences' Commoweal 105:12, 16 June 1978. In that article Gustafson observes that few people writing as 'ethicists' give explicit theological authorisation for their ethical perspectives. Most write as 'ethicists' in a manner that the relation of their moral discourse to any specific theological view is opaque. Gustafson notes that Christian ethicists try to justify the importance of theology in terms of the light it may cast on issues related to science and medicine. But Gustafson goes on to confess, 'I worked for years on a book, "Can Ethics be Christian?", with the nagging sense that most persons who answer in an unambiguous affirmative would not be interested in my supporting arguments . . . for those who believe the answer is negative the question itself is not sufficiently important to bother about.' Niebuhr's ethics illustrates this problem.

Niebuhr's social vision articulated in *Moral Man: Immoral Society*, lacked any theological justification. It is this issue that he sought to address in his book, *The interpretation of Christian Ethics*. In this book, reflecting the tradition of theological liberalism, Niebuhr suggests that Jesus is the embodiment of love. This love is the impossible possibility that stands as the criterion, the judge, of all human efforts to achieve justice. In Niebuhr's view liberalism may have had a too optimistic view of human nature and its potential, on the other hand classical orthodoxy had a too pessimistic view of its possibilities. Consequently Niebuhr sought to hold on to a dialectical view of the relationship between the impossible possibility of love as the criterion for understanding human attempts to achieve justice in the earthly realm.

Niebuhr's most complete articulation of this dialectical relationship between love and justice is to be found in his Gifford lectures at the University of Edinburgh in 1941 and 1944; these were published as a two volume work *The Nature and Destiny of Man*. Drawing on elements in the thought of Kierkegaard and Augustine, Niebuhr depicts the human condition as dominated by sin. We are creatures ridden with anxiety grounded in our mortality and our capacity for self transcendence. In this situation human beings seek ways of over coming this anxiety, they seek to secure their existence against living with the burden of the knowledge of their finitude. Yet humans attempt to accomplish this result in precisely the opposite. The individual and collective neuroses become pathological in the form of all against all, the law of the survival of the fittest. In pride humans seek to create a world in which no one can question our superiority or by means of the obverse of pride, dissipation, people seek to lose the terrible knowledge of their mortality, the limits of which is so threatening.

This account given by Neibuhr of sin and the human condition earned him the reputation of being orthodox. Yet Niebuhr was anything but orthodox. Niebuhr's doctrine of sin became the means for him to develop a Protestant natural theology. He was fond of quoting the *London Times* to the effect that the only Christian doctrine which was empirically verifiable was that of original sin. This, of course, is false since we can only know sin as the other side of the action by which God forgives us our sin. It is only in the light of the cross of Christ that we can come to an understanding of the nature of human cupidity. But Niebuhr had a minimal Christology. For him Christ stands on the edge of history not in it; for by Christ he means the symbolic exemplification of self-sacrificial love that judges all human attempts at just action.

Accordingly what Christians should seek to enact is not love but justice. By justice Niebuhr means the most equitable balance of power between the competing interests that constitute any given society. So a just society is one that allows for the free interplay between interest groups in such a way that avoids hegemonic control by any one group or individual. In this aspect of Niebuhr's thought we see the justice of Hauerwas's complaint that in Niebuhr the subject of Christian ethics is America!

The net result of Niebuhr's criticism of the social gospel movement and the constructive statement of his own views as to the possibility of just human actions is that Christian ethics after Niebuhr no longer talked about Jesus but justice. No longer do Christians seek to Christianise society after the fashion of Rauschenbusch and the 'social gospel'. Now the Christian's task is to secure as much justice as possible in the situations in which they find themselves. Such justice as is achieved must be kept in constant tension with the impossible ideal of love in order to ensure that such justice as is achieved does not become identified with the *status quo*. This is the analytical task of Christian ethics which no longer need concern itself with theological and/or Christological questions and issues. Christian ethics after Niebuhr become social science with a difference. And like social science it becomes difficult to distinguish Christian ethics from journalism.

It seems to me that the task group has two broad alternatives which it may persue in developing its theological position with respect to the church's responsibility for the provision of health care in the form of the hospitals it presently sponsors. We may either adopt a variant of the Niebuhrian methodology or the more difficult path which arises from an analysis of the issues in terms of the question, 'What am I to do'?, 'I am to do what I am become', act in accordance with what it has *been given to me to be* as a member of the Body of Christ. This latter approach will necessarily involve an examination of the doctrine of the church and its mission in terms of the nature of its life in Christ.

Agathon: A Journal of Ethics and Value in the Modern World, Vol 9/2022

The Church's Responsibility for the World: A Reformed Perspective

A paper prepared for the Uniting Church in Australia, Queensland Synod Hospital Task Group constituted to report on the issue of the Church's involvement in the provision of Health Care in the State October 1997

Gordon Watson

The Context and the Question . . .

The following contribution by the 'theological' sub-committee of the hospital task group attempts to bring to bear the church's understanding of its faith upon the issue of the church's involvement in health care through the specific form of its ownership of hospitals. In order to appreciate the complexity of the issues involved it is important that the *context* in which the question is being discussed is agreed and secondly, that the *question* that is being examined is understood.

The context in which the issue of the Church's relationship to health care, in particular hospitals, is raised is one which mitigates against the church's actions being understood. The contemporary context in which the church is set is conditioned by the movement in European thought known as the 'Enlightenment' of the eighteenth century and by its consequences for our present self understanding.

The major consequence has been to the creation of a mental world with which we become familiar before we can articulate its meaning. It is a world in which the 'knowing subject' defines external reality in terms of 'objective facts'. These 'objective facts' are 'value free', since they are the same for every reasonable person. These 'facts' are understood to be the determinate of truth. With unprecedented zeal the Enlightenment proposed to explain the world as something that is without purpose. The idea of purpose, as of any other 'value', is understood to belong to the 'subjective' sphere and is to be excluded as a determinate of truth on the precise ground of it being a subjective variable. This dichotomy between fact and value, the explanation of everything in terms of antecedent causes according to a mechanistic model of reality and the relegation of values to the privatised sphere of the individual subject is the 'Enlightenment's' most characteristic and influential legacy. With characteristic zeal the Enlightenment thinkers pursued the idea of the methodological elimination of purpose from the study of the human; to the extent that it is assumed in our culture to be a universally valid maxim.

The public world, the world of economic relationships, is the world of facts; these are the same for everybody irrespective of their private values. The private world of values is that sphere where each is free to choose their own meaning which may interpret the facts. *The question then arises* whether Christian truth claims about human persons and their place in the world is simply another voice in a universal debating chamber; a night in which all cats are grey. Or whether there is a way of expressing Christian truth claims as public truth. That is to say claims which refer to the public world of facts, for example, the nature of the human person; that these claims have a particular form and a structure since their intelligibility is derived from, since it is grounded in, the nature of a world made to be related to a personal God.

The Church's relationship to the world

We cannot understand the relationship between the Church and the world as between two different realities, the 'sacred' and the 'secular'. There is not two realities but one which is defined by the action of God in God's self revelation in Jesus Christ. He it is Who defines the nature of the church and the world in their relationship and difference, since it is He Who is both the Creator Word and the Incarnate Word who reconciles the world to God; fulfils the divine purpose for creation.

We begin to see what this means when we turn to explaining the significance of the relationship between creation and covenant in the Bible.

Israel believed as God had acted in relationship to them, so it was also true of God's relationship to the world; God leads the world, like God led Israel, out of the threatening watery chaos and brings forth the dry land as a cosmos; giving it to humans as their habitation as God gave the land of Canaan to God's people as their home. Stamped by their saving experience of God through their exodus from Egypt and the gift of the land, Israel's understanding of the world as God's creation entailed that they saw the world not as a self enclosed series of random events featuring an eternal cycle of ultimate meaninglessness, but on the contrary just as their history was understood to be guided by God's redemptive purpose, so also the world has a history, a purpose. Consequently Israel historicised the creation myths which they borrowed from their cultural and ethnic neighbours, they turned them into accounts which related not abstract and timeless ideas but the history of the world and Israel's place as God's people in that world.

God's presence and activity in the world, as in relationship to Israel, is one which preserves it in being and safeguards it against a return to the chaos of disorder over which God triumphed in the beginning. Just as God preserves Israel and safeguards it as God's people from the threat of annihilation by natural catastrophes such as the desiccating wilderness and the flood: so too the powers of negation which reach into the life of the world are reminders of the fragility of the world's existence, dependent every moment that it exists on God's gracious care.

But the faith of Israel as expressed in the writings of the Old Testament do not merely testify to the Exodus experience and the consequent faith in God as the Creator of the world; they also witness to the hope of a future in which creation will be renewed by God's action which will reveal the final triumph of God over all that inimical to God's purposes and therefore negates the life of God's creature.

While this vision of a renewed creation echoes the experience of the initial exodus from Egypt it goes beyond simply recalling that fact. Isaiah 48:12 says those that go out will neither hunger nor thirst: their path is easy because all barriers have been cleared away. Isaiah 49:11 Nature itself will participate in this future liberation of God's people. The mountains will break forth into rejoicing and the trees will clap their hands. Isaiah 49:13, 55:12. Waters shall spring forth in the wilderness and streams in the desert. Isaiah 35:6. All nations shall see this and know that the God of Israel is the God of their salvation. Isaiah 41:11, 42:17, 45:14*ff*. This eschatological vision fulfils the original creation. The exodus out of the chaos of slavery and the present world existing under the threat of chaos, preserved from the waters above the firmament and the encroaching threat of the sea by God's providential care, will be followed by the transfiguration of creation in the unveiled presence of God.

It was Israel's understanding of itself as called and chosen by God through it's particular historical experience that it came to recognise its gracious God as the Creator of the world. The classic expression of God's covenanted relationship with Israel is found in Exodus 20:1–2.

This aspect of Israel's experience of God has important implication for our understanding of the nature of created reality. The world created by God in freedom is not simply a contingent entity but is so made as to be the sphere in which God can establish a personal relationship with the creature. Thus the being of the world is one in which the personal relationship willed by God with the creature has priority over the impersonal.[1]

To know the God of Israel is to know that ones existence and that of the world is created for relationship with the other; God and other human beings. This is the fundamental grammar of creation and it is seen already in the covenant established between God and Israel. The law which is given to Israel as a sign of the covenanted relationship has its basic character configured in terms of God's claim upon Israel in their relationship with God and the neighbour. What has been called the two tables of the law indicate that God's purposes for Israel are focused in their relationship with God and their relationship with each other. The important Hebrew word *Shalom* (peace) is a word used in the context of the covenant relationship of God with Israel. *Shalom* (peace) is realised in a community. The people of Israel were primarily a community not a state. When the State, the monarchy and the priesthood became 'powers', this was detrimental to Israel as God's covenanted community. These led to divisions, discrimination, oppression and poverty, the absence of *Shalom* (peace).

(a) The creation narratives depict human beings as essentially related to God, to each other and the earth. These relationships are in turn inter-related. What happens in humans relationship with God affects their relationship with each other and the earth. The primary relatedness of which the Bible speaks is that by which humans are referred to God. This relationship is constitutive of what being human means. They are related to God by the sheer fact of their existence. God does not first create humans and then relate to them. The decision to create

---

1. See J Zizioulas, 'Human capacity and incapacity', in *Scottish Journal of Theology*, (1975): 401–444.

human beings in relationship to God is made by God prior to their creation, Genesis 1:26. Genesis 5 and 10 indicate in their recitation of the *'toledoth'* of human generations after Adam and after Noah that the relatedness of human beings to God extends to all generations, to all people and races and to all time. Human beings remain related to God even and precisely when they are shown to be hostile to God.

God's will is revealed to humans in the form of God's command which means that the relationship they have with God is not a fate which overtakes them by the mere fact that they exist. It implies that the relationship between God and the creature is established by God in freedom and thus entails an act of will. Humans may or may not remain in communion with God. So God calls them to account. Genesis 3: 'who told you you were naked?', 'where are you?' 'what have you done?' The human creature has the right of reply, as distinct from animals, such as the serpent.

Not only are human beings accountable to God for their relationship to God but also for their actions in relation to each other. Genesis 9 implies that anyone who murders another human being has to answer to God for the blood that is shed

The accountability we find in the biblical story is not the law of retribution as is found in the Greek tragedians account of relationships between gods and human beings. There the transgressors are punished by an inevitable fate. In the biblical account the relationship between God and human beings is one which involves a freedom that is characteristic of inter-personal relationships. God decides personally on the consequences of human sin; God's mind can change, God can repent. God can choose Godself to be answerable for human beings wrong doing. God chooses to be answerable for the blood of the fratricide Cain.

The Bible sees human dignity and worth grounded in a relationship established by God with human beings prior to and independent of any human action in the act of creation. Although this relationship is corrupted by human sin it is upheld and confirmed by God's action in both judgement and grace.

Jesus Christ and His Messianic Community

The transition from the people of God under the old covenant to the people of God under the new covenant was through the action of God in the fulfilment of the history of Israel in the birth, life, death and resurrection of Israel's Messiah, Jesus the Christ.

The Christian church can never overlook the fact which John states ever so plainly,

> John 4:22—'You worship what you do not know; we worship what we know, for salvation is from the Jews.'

This too is the intent of St Paul's argument in Romans 11:17ff.

In the first act of Jesus' public ministry Jesus submits Himself to the baptism of repentance proclaimed by John the Baptist. This was a baptism of repentance for the remission of sins. He who is the holy Son of God voluntarily identifies himself in the first act of his public ministry with the sin of Israel God's covenanted people. It is at this moment that Jesus' action is publicly confirmed by the Father in the sending of the Holy Spirit to rest upon Jesus. He who is ever one with the Father and the Spirit, who is God by nature and does not need to be given the Spirit, nevertheless submits Himself, in identification with the flesh of fallen Israel to this dependency upon the gift and promise of God. (*Cf* Phil 2:7–11) Jesus thus receives the Spirit not for His own sake but for the sake of all those whom He represents in the flesh He assumed from Mary, all Israel.

In receiving the Spirit vicariously, within the fallen flesh of Israel He had assumed from Mary, Jesus assumes responsibility before God for what God finds Israel to be in relation to God's self—He assumes responsibility for Israel as the breakers of God's covenant! He thus bears within Himself the contradiction between God's holiness and the rebellion of human beings against God; this in the form of the flesh of Israel. Jesus' Baptism was thus His consecration to the whole course of His life and ministry as the incarnate Son of God. It prefigures in dramatic fashion the intimate connection between Jesus life and death. His death was not the unhappy ending of an otherwise happy religious life. Jesus' death was the fulfilment of the purpose of His obedience as the Son of God. His obedience was to be this one thing; God in the *flesh*: with all that that involves in terms of His being both rejected by God and by His fellow human beings.

It is this connection between Jesus incarnation and His cross, the incarnation and the atonement, that provides the basis for understanding the continuity and discontinuity between the Old and the New Covenants.

Under the Old Testament or Covenant God provided in a unilateral fashion the means of Israel's response in the context of its alienation and estrangement from God. Thus through the cult and the Law God promises God's self to be Israel's savour and Lord. The blood of the sacrifice on the day of Atonement[2] is God's gift and offering which God provides for the people. The prohibition on the eating of blood is precisely because the blood of all created things is equivalent to their life which is God's, as the Creator and author of all life. Enshrined in the Law is God's promise. 'I will be your God and you shall be my people.'[3] In the gift of the Law God promises God's self to Israel, takes responsibility for them as the recipients of the Law and therefore as the breakers of the Law. In the Cult and the Law we thus see the provisional form of God's purpose in establishing the covenant with God's people. They were the God provided means of a continuing relationship with a sinful people, and through this people with the world of humanity. The Cult and the Law were the God provided means of God remaining just in and for God's self and also remaining faithful to a faithless people at one and the same time.

> In Jesus Christ the long relationship between God and Israel under the covenant comes to an end, in the sense of it being fulfilled. In Him the Word and will of God is actualised in human existence.

Jesus Himself is the form of *the New Covenant* since He *is* the New Covenant. He is both in Himself the God who draws near to sinful humanity in judgement and forgiveness, bearing in Himself the cost of human redemption, but also at the same time He is he Human Being who responds to God's faithfulness with fidelity and trust, love and obedience: God's will is translated into human flesh, as the cult and the law testified under the Old Covenant. The Covenant and its institutions, the cult and the law, are now no longer aspects of an external relationship between God and human beings but are identical with the being and life of the Son of God.

---

2. Leviticus 23*ff.*
3. *Cf* Exodus 6:7; Jeremiah 7:23.

We are therefore to think of Jesus' whole life, death and resurrection, as He passes through every stage of human development, that there takes place in Him a reconstitution or re-creation of our human being in relationship to God. God in Christ recreates the relationship between God's self and the creature in such a manner that it is not something that takes place, as it were, above our heads in some external way, but God penetrates to the depths of our human condition and bears in God's own self the cost of our redemption. He is, as St. John the Baptist proclaimed St John 1:29 'the *Lamb of God who takes away the sin of the world!*'

This does not happen by means of some forensic conjuring trick. Jesus, as God's own Son, bears in Himself the godforsakenness of the human condition. From the first act of His public ministry there is marked out the way of the cross and the resurrection; as through His obedient penitence in behalf of sinners and His healing the diseased humanity which clung to Him at every turn, He presses His way forward to the goal of His life and embraces the cross as its fulfilment: *Cf* Hebrews 2:10–17; 5:7–9. In Jesus then the Covenant is fulfilled, both from the side of the God who gives and promises Godself to the creature and from the human side whereby there is found in Him an obedient human 'Amen', to the judgement and the love of God.

If this is the case, that we must consider the New Covenant to be not something external to who Jesus Christ is for our sake but as identical with who He wills to be for us; this means that the church cannot be a holy society dedicated to perpetuating the memory of a great religious teacher but exists as a community 'in Christ' (*Cf* 2 Cor 5:17; Gal 3:26; 5:6; Eph 2:10; Col 1:4; 1:24; 1Thess 4:16; Heb 3:14.) The church's life inheres in the person of Jesus Christ the Son of God.

The Relationship Between the Church and God's Promised Future for Creation

The claim is made by the gospel of St John that the incarnate Son of God is the universal Word of God who was in the beginning with God and without whom nothing was created that came to be. This Word of God is the foundation of the created intelligibility of the world. The *logos* is the light which enlightens every person who is born into the world. This *logos* became flesh: *'flesh' in the Genesis narrative is a relational term binding humankind together as one kin as well as linking humankind with all living creatures.*

At the same time the word 'flesh' establishes the basic distinction between God and human creatures. By the incarnation the condescension of God identifies God's own self with 'flesh'. In the John's Gospel, 'flesh' does not mean humanity in any abstract neutral sense but humanity in organised opposition to God. The faithfulness of God is such that God takes personal responsibility for the human creature in its turning away from God by assuming its flesh in the person of God's Son

The incarnation of the Son of God indicates the manner in which God wills to reconstitute the relationship between Godself, the creature and between human beings and other creatures. In contrast to Adam Christ did not strive to be 'like God' though He was by nature God He 'emptied Himself', Philippians 2; He let go of His natural God likeness in order to make Himself one with Adam's flesh. The upward striving of Adam is reversed by the condescension of God. And in this self humiliation of God consists the exaltation of the human creature.

In contrast to the first Adam Christ, 'trusts every word that proceeds from the mouth of God', rather than listen to the suggestion of the tempter: Matthew 4:11.

In contrast to the first Adam Christ did not seek to justify Himself over against God and other human beings, He remains silent before Pilate. Matthew 26:63; Mark 14:61; *cf* Acts 8:32. In this way he bears eloquent testimony to the fact that He takes responsibility for the condition of the flesh with which by His incarnation He identifies Himself. Consequently, He is accurately described by John the Baptist as 'the lamb of God who takes away the sin of the world' John 1:29.

He makes Himself one with sinners by submitting at the hand of John the Baptist to a 'baptism of repentance for the forgiveness of sins'. He 'fulfils all righteousness' by placing Himself in the wrong before God: Matthew 3:13–14. St Paul says Jesus Christ becomes a 'curse' Galatians 3:13.

Unlike Cain He sheds no innocent blood but allows His innocent blood to be shed. His blood unlike that of Abel's' does not cry out for vengeance but for mercy Hebrews 12:24.

Unlike Cain's descendent Lamech Genesis 4:16–24., who would avenge seventy times for an injury, He prays for forgiveness for those who take His life; He instructs His disciples to forgive seventy times seven.

The narrative of Genesis 1–11 helps in the appreciation of the New Testament conviction that in the person of Jesus Christ there is present in the world *God's work of recreation whereby all the dismal consequences of the archetypal human temptation to be 'like God' are reversed*. The transgression of the first Adam is reversed by the obedience of the second Adam and there comes into being the Head of a new humanity in the form of the Body of Christ which is the herald of the coming new creation.

Christ is not only a son of Adam as the Word made flesh He is also at one and the same time the Son of God. Genesis 5 indicates one of the meanings of the *imago Dei* of Genesis 1 is the relationship between a human father and a human son.

> Genesis 5:3—When Adam had lived one hundred thirty years, he became the father of a son in his likeness, according to his image, and named him Seth.

There is a similar relationship indicated in the New Testament when Jesus is described by St Paul as the *eikon* or image of God: Colossians 1:15; 2 Corinthians 4:4. Christ as the Image of God shares a unique relationship with the Father as the true Image and Likeness of God; but He also shares a relationship in His flesh with all humankind. He is the image and likeness of Adam, sinful flesh.

> Romans 8:3—For God has done what the law, weakened by the flesh, could not do: by sending his own Son in the *likeness* of sinful flesh, and to deal with sin, he condemned sin in the flesh,

Christ's unique being as the image and likeness of God and human beings is for *the purpose of re-establishing human beings in their created purpose in relationship to God and each other*. So Christ invites His disciples to enter into that unique relationship He shares with the Father by placing this name upon their lips in the prayer which He gives them: Matthew 6:9. *Cf* Galatians 4:6 'God sent the Spirit of His Son into our hearts, crying, "Abba"! Father.'

This restoration of human communion with God and each other is identified with the person of Jesus Christ; the truth of the restored relationship between God and the creature inheres in the person of Jesus Christ. There has been minted out in His flesh by His earthly obedience a new human being so that at every stage of our human development from conception to death and beyond the grave our relationship with God is set upon a new footing as a result of the presence in the world of the Son of God.

It is in the Holy Spirit that humans come to know and participate the renewed truth of their relationship with God and each other as members of the Body of Christ in Baptism. This Spirit is mediated by the risen Jesus Christ since He first received the Spirit, not for His own sake but for ours. As Son of God He did not need the Spirit in order to be one with God the Father, He is ever one with the Father and the Spirit. *But He receives the Spirit*: He is conceived by the Spirit in Mary's womb, He receives the Spirit in His Baptism as the first act of His public ministry, He accomplishes His mighty works by the Spirit, He offers Himself to the Father on the cross through the eternal Spirit Hebrews 9:14, and is raised from the dead by the Spirit. Thus the ascended Christ unites His Body the Church with Himself by the Spirit in whom, once and for all, He sanctified our flesh. Thus those who are united with Christ are set on a way by which they are transformed and transfigured into His likeness.

> 2 Corinthians 3:18—And all of us, with unveiled faces, seeing the glory of the Lord as though reflected in a mirror, are being transformed into the same image from one degree of glory to another; for this comes from the Lord, the Spirit.

> *The critical function of the humanity of Jesus Christ the Incarnate Son of God in expressing the teleology of human existence; it's created purpose.*

By His incarnation the Son of God minted out in our humanity the material basis of a renewed human being adapted to the truth of the relationships in which our humanity is grounded: in relationship to God and in relationship to each other. Jesus Christ is Himself then the one place in the material universe of time and space where the truth of God's personal being is adapted by God's own action to the logical and verbal patterns of our human existence.

The basis of John Calvin's claim for the relationship between creation and redemption, allowing for the continuities and discontinuities presupposed by God's act of reconciliation, is the fact that God's relationship to the world is mediated in creation and redemption by the one Christ. The relationship God establishes with the creature is one which relates to Christ and the Spirit who 'accommodate' themselves in humility to the lowly estate of the creature, in order to raise it to God's glory. This being the case then *the created structures of human reason and experience become the means God uses to communicate Himself in acts of gracious union and communion.*[4]

This voluntary self emptying of the Son of God is the basis of the reconstituting act whereby through the obedience of the second Adam the wilful disobedience of the first Adam is replaced in the humanity of Christ for our sake. Likewise Calvin believes that Christ's humanity was not relinquished by His Ascension. For Christ did not need exaltation as the Son of God, He is ever one with the Father and the Spirit, He was and is exalted for our sake. He never ceased to be God and rule the universe, He was exalted according to His manifestation for sinners as their High Priest.[5] God the Father has appointed Christ 'heir of all things', Hebrews 1:2, according to his accommodation to our lowliness not according to His eternal divinity.

> Calvin's use of what later became known as the *extra Calvinisticum* ensured that he was able to give theological significance to the relative ethical judgments that we are called upon to make as christians, and non-Christians, without compromising the free grace of the gospel. The relationship between God and the creature established in Christ is one which takes account of the relativities of the human situation. This situation is mediated by the person of Jesus Christ the Mediator who in himself accommodates and continues to accommodate Himself through the Holy Spirit to the created modes of our existence as the means whereby He wills to exercise His rule in the church and the world. *The focus of theological coherence for Calvin is thus this worldly and cosmic in its nature and scope.*

In the light of the cosmic scope of the biblical witness to God's economy of salvation as fulfilled in Jesus Christ it is demonstrated that one cannot understand the relationship between the church

---

4. See ED Willis, *Calvin's Catholic Christology: The Role of the So-Called 'extra Calvinisticum' in Calvin's Theology* (Leiden: EJ Brill, 1966).

5. J Calvin, *Institutes* 2.13.2. *Cf* Commentary Hebrews 5:7.

and the world as between two different realities, the 'sacred' and the 'secular'. There is not two realities but one which is defined by the action of God in God's self revelation in Jesus Christ. He it is Who defines the nature of the church and the world in their relationship and difference, since it is He Who is both the Creator Word and the Incarnate Word who reconciles the world to God; He fulfils the divine purpose for creation.[6]

The question then for the church in the context of its life in the world is not whether but how by its life and work it should witness in both word and deed to the truth of its life in Jesus Christ as Lord of the church and the world. The church's establishment of hospitals in the middle-ages and its continued involvement in this form of health care indicates the Christian conviction that it is God's will to renew human beings in the context of the cosmic scope of God's reconciling purpose. Hospitals proclaim the church's commitment to this holy purpose of God; to renew creation and safeguard it against all that is inimical to its created purpose.

The issue then is not whether the church should or should not be involved in serving the needs of people who are sick but whether the present way it performs this task is the most appropriate given the needs of the community in which it is placed.

Second, the church must ask itself, not simply from the point of view of efficiency whether this task should be carried out in cooperation with other Christian churches. The church has this mandate not as an accidental characteristic but an essential characteristic of its life in and for the world.

---

6.   *Cf* D Bonhoeffer, *Ethics* (London: SCM Press, 1955), 55*ff*.

Agathon: A Journal of Ethics and Value in the Modern World, Vol 9/2022

Catholic Identity: Lost, and Found

Anthony Kelly CSsR

Catholic Identity: what is the question? 'Exploding or Expanding', or, perhaps a little closer to the bone, 'Catholic Identity—living off it, or, for it'? Then, pointing more to the solution in the long run, How to put the '. . . holic' back into the 'Cat-holic'? Well, we opted for the general title, leaving it open to you to entitle what follows as you see fit!

True, 'Catholic Identity: Lost and Found' is hardly a catchy title. But a loss of identity is an unsettling experience being felt the world over. We have seen whole empires, the British and the Soviet, wane and retire from the scene. Our own country is renegotiating its identity in the world of Asia. The Catholic Church, the oldest institution in Western history, had to find itself when confronted by the awesome might of the Roman Empire, only to see that empire collapse and wither away, just as the kingdoms and empires centuries later came to an end. We think we have identity problems today, but history would suggest that an 'identity crisis' is something like a permanent state. Post-Christendom Europe itself is struggling to find a united and inclusive identity over these decades past. And of course those 'masters of the universe' whom the world most trusted to preside over the global financial system have left us all aghast at the silliness and shameful short-term greed behind it all. In the great wash of our time, cultures, political parties, whole nations and peoples are being tossed about. The pain has been particular great with indigenous peoples. Yet, in some ways, the patience, courage and hope evident in our own indigenous Australians may well become an example for all peoples and cultures as we move into the future.

When we address the question of Catholic identity, we are involved in something more challenging than recovering a furtive sock in laundry dryer. There is level of deep sadness with the loss or disaffection of so many who once walked with us on the way of Catholic faith. If Catholic identity is to be affirmed and invigorated, imaginative spiritual, pastoral and theological responses will be necessary—in regard to the disaffected, the laicized, the divorced, the alienated, and the forgotten generally. Grief must be suffered with patience and hope, but the prospect of an increasing Eucharistic starvation throughout the Church resulting from the diminishing number of priests strikes at the heart. If the Eucharist is focal sacrament of Catholic identity, we must pray for something to happen here, be it through a flowering of vocations as we know them, the discovery of new vocations and new kinds of ordination—or whatever else—that the Eucharistic identity of the Catholic people will not suffer any terminal loss.

There are the negatives and the positives. We may recall, for instance, the World Youth Day held in Sydney some years ago, when, from different perspectives either as participants or somewhat detached observers, we contemplated that remarkable event. But, more generally, as our eminent respondents will make clear, discussion of 'Catholic Identity' is cropping up everywhere—not only in those huge, enterprising sectors of Catholic Education, Health Care, Social Work, and so forth, but also even in a understanding of what is a Catholic University itself! Clearly, it is a time of regrouping if we are to be what we claim to be. To consider who we are and what we are called to be is, admittedly, to experience enormous pressures. I recall reading of a strange experiment performed by the US General Electric Company in 1960. The scientists subjected a couple of ounces of peanut butter to enormous pressure under extreme heat—a million pounds per square inch. The result? No, not just a squashed lump of peanut butter, for it was now so carbonized that it had become tiny diamonds. In the pressure of our times, our deepest Catholic identity can feel like squashed peanut butter. My hope is that we are becoming diamonds in our way, tough in the ability to resist what might erode who we are, yet sparkling with the light.

Given the extent of current discussion and the immensity of the topic, it would be pretentious on my part to aim for anything other than contributing some small ingredient to the mix. Accordingly, I offer to your consideration just four remarks as background for all the discussion that must go on:

1. Watching our words;
2. Dimension of Catholic Identity

1. Watching our Words

Any talk of Catholic identity is, first of all, part of a much larger conversation; indeed, it contributes to the long conversation that the Church embodies, as it testifies to God's own Word becoming flesh in order to enter into the unending conversation we call 'human history'. In that world of communication, Catholic faith today thinks of itself in more conversational and dialogical terms compared to more defensive times of persecution and conflict. It reaches out to Christian peoples everywhere; and, indeed, to all good people in all the varieties of their religious searching and finding. In our present exploration, I would like to include from the beginning all other Churches and communities and religious traditions which might happily associate themselves with our examination of authentic Catholic identity, even if there are limits beyond which they cannot go. Still, something wonderful has happened in the Catholic Church when it recognised that its identity is far more porous and alive than solid granite; and that the ecology of its life included, in ways that are still struggling for expression, the presence of what Catholics regard as authentic elements of the Church in other Christian communities. And, of course, we recognize the transforming presence of Christ's paschal mystery and the workings of the Spirit in all lives. Theologians continue to discuss those words of the Council on how the fullness of Church 'subsists' in the sacramentally and institutionally structured communion of the Catholic Church in communion with the Bishop of Rome—a seemingly technical point on the use of a rare word instead of the straight out 'is'. But it provokes us to reflect on how Vatican II felt impelled to acknowledge more clearly the larger communion of grace in which the Lord of the Church is acting. It is as though the dynamism of Catholic faith must admit a two-way traffic: it is centripetal in that it is ever coming back to an enduring scriptural, sacramental, doctrinal and institutional centre. It is centrifugal, as it moves out, on the path of friendships, reconciliation, dialogical events and collaborative enterprises that turn us outward to the limitless domain of the Spirit; and invite us upward into the Father's house of many rooms.

I have to admit that I am inclined to avoid the word, 'Catholicism'. It is not, first of all, a Catholic word, and, as far as I know, never appears in any official Church documents. It was a word employed in French Ultramontane contexts in the first half of the nineteenth century, though it had some currency in English from the seventeenth century. It gives the impression, like all 'isms', of an ideology, of a closed system of principles and positions. It represents an attempt to reduce the personal *fides catholica* ('the Catholic faith'), or the communal *ecclesia catholica* ('the Catholic Church') to a system of ideas—one more 'ism' in a world of then burgeoning 'isms'—that is far too rigid in the dialogical context of the Church today. We are not 'catholicists', proponents of a particular ideological system, but Catholics, committed to follow Christ in confessing 'the catholic faith', as the Catholic people who make up the 1.3 billion members of the Catholic Church. In other words, 'Catholicism' does not suggest change, development, outreach, let alone evoke the full dimension of the Catholic faith with an engagement of mind, heart, imagination and moral responsibility.

While we're at it, I am also averse to using the term 'Roman Catholic'—except to designate the Catholic people of Rome, who, incidentally, seem to hear of Vatican pronouncements rather later than we do here in Australia. I know the term, 'Roman Catholic' was imposed by the British government in the context of Catholic emancipation in England, but, though often used in the US, it was never part of the European, Irish and Australian usage. I would prefer to say that I, for instance, am an Australian Catholic of the Latin rite, in communion with the Bishop of Rome, and a member of an international religious community. Admittedly, ecumenical etiquette may recommend against any rigidity on this point, since other Christian communities may wish to use the word 'catholic' of themselves. Fair enough; but, as I say, I fail to see why we Catholics are the only ones who must have an identity crisis!

Interestingly, despite the frequent tendency to translate the word, 'catholic', as simply as 'universal', the early Church chose to use, not the Latin word, *universalis*, but a Latinised Greek word, *catholicus*: *Credo in unam, sanctam, catholicam et apostolicam ecclesiam. Universalis* would have connoted something immense, but still homogenous and uniform throughout. *Catholica* implies something different, a living, communing, expanding reality, with the whole in each part, and each part functioning within the living whole, in a communicating plurality of ecclesial expressions. The many rites— nineteen by one count: Latin, Ukrainian, Chaldean, Maronite, and so forth, are an often unnoticed witness to a unity in diversity, just as these promise a possible way of conceiving of church unity in future. Something like this is implied in Benedict XVI's recent Apostolic Constitution, *Anglicanorum Coetibus* (November 2009) which allows for corporate reception of Anglican communities into the Catholic Church, though keeping much of their traditions through the setting up of 'ordinariates' within the present Church structure.

Vatican II imagined catholicity in a particularly dynamic and diversified manner. The dynamism consists in it being a 'gift of the Lord whereby the Catholic Church tends efficaciously and constantly to recapitulate the whole of humanity with all its riches, under Christ the head, and in the unity of the Spirit' (*Lumen Gentium*, #13). A kind of ecological diversity is suggested when it states, 'In virtue of this catholicity each individual parts brings its particular gifts to the other parts and to the whole Church, so that the whole and the individual parts are enriched by the mutual sharing of gifts and the striving of all for the fullness of unity . .' (*Lumen Gentium*, #13). The council was careful to present the Church as a diversified unity of the local with the universal. The pope, as Bishop of Rome, was understood to preside over the whole assembly of charity so as to protect legitimate differences and to prevent them from becoming divisive (*Lumen Gentium*, #13)—a rather large job description. The cooperation of the local churches, under their respective bishops, was viewed as 'particularly splendid evidence of the undivided Church' (*Lumen Gentium*, #23). Similarly, the Church's missionary activity must respect the requirements of genuine catholicity. The Church proclaims the Gospel because it is impelled by 'the innermost requirements of her own catholicity' (*Ad Gentes*, #1), to 'perfect its own catholic unity by expanding it' (*Ad Gentes*, #6). In so doing, the Catholic vocation is to heal, ennoble and to perfect all the authentic values present in the traditions and cultures of various peoples (*Ad Gentes*, #9, 22).

On this point of Catholicity I have two further remarks. The first one deals the need to understand Catholic faith as a movement within history. There is no point in speaking about the Catholic Church, let alone Catholic identity, if we have no sense of the history of Catholic identity over the last two millennia, and the long line of apostles, evangelists, saints, doctors, pastors, martyrs, missionaries and mystics, visionaries, reformers and religious founders who populate that great communion reaching beyond time, and into which each of us, and every generation, is being gathered. To have such a sense of corporate communion extending in and beyond time is difficult in the modern amnesiac context, when history is general, and our Catholic history in particular, are notably lacking in educational curricula, even in Catholic schools and universities.[1] A state of amnesia is not notably creative, and it is ill-advised to press someone suffering a memory-loss to be more precise about their identity! Without its sense of history, Catholic identity becomes at best a flimsy tissue of opinions and convictions.

Second, there is the matter of catholicity as universality. Here, Catholic identity is not realised by modeling itself on the world-wide web, or on systems of global communication (and surveillance) more generally; nor on global governance of the UN kind, let alone on that kind of lamentable globalisation that tends to standardize consumerist aspirations of everyone on the planet. Macdonalds does it better, and Coca Cola was there first. Mere planetary universality in aspiration or effect is not what the Catholic identity is about. Of course, Catholic identity has a large global reach, but the horizon of its universality accords with the intentionality of faith, hope and love. If God so loves the world, how can anyone be left out of the concerns of the Church? If God wishes all to be saved and to come to the knowledge of the truth, this implies an ecclesial communication designed to represent and make available to all, in word, deed and sacrament, the saving mystery of God's will. If all things are made in Christ and for him, and if in him all things hold together (*cf* Col 1:15–18), there is a wholeness, a 'cat-holicity' that is not the homogenization of a system or a universal product or design, but that of the personal love of Christ for each and everyone. We cannot corner the market in regard to limitless gifts of God, nor administer the infinite treasure of Christ. In the universe of grace, we are all sinners; and, as called out of ourselves to be something infinitely more, it is only by reason of a gift coming from beyond anything we are or can do in ourselves.

2. Dimensions of Catholic Identity

Within the focal identity of the Church in Christ, there is a kind of composite: there is Peter the Rock; and Jesus saying 'you are Peter

---

1. For a good resource, see Thomas E Woods, *How the Catholic Church Built Western Civilization* (Washington, DC: Regnery, 2005).

and on this rock I will build my church' (Mt 16:18). But there is the presence of Mary in the Church is a vital part of Catholic identity, and a source of lively ecumenical dialogue. For example, there is the Anglican-Catholic statement a couple of years back, *Mary: Grace and Hope in Christ* (2004);[2] and then a US document produced in the dialogue between Catholics and Evangelicals this year, *Do Whatever he tells you: the Blessed Virgin Mary in Christian Faith and Life*. But there is Mary, too, as Jesus address his Mother from the cross, 'Woman, here is your son', and speaks to the beloved disciple, representing the whole Church, 'Here is your mother' (Jn 19:26–27). It seems to me that Catholic identity today is calling for the blending of the organizational Petrine rock-like structure of the Church with the Marian maternal nurturing aspects of *sancta mater ecclesia*. Mary embodies the identity of the Church, and shapes its vocation, with her words, 'Do whatever he tells you' (Jn 2:5). You could, of course, add the Pauline dimension, the summons to continual conversion and outreach embodied in the great Apostle. Then, there is the Johannine depth of communion—in the words of Jesus' prayer, 'that they may be one, just as we are one' (Jn 17:22). For us Catholics, at least of an older generation, the challenge is to so understand our Catholic identity more as a hologram in which each of these dimensions interweave. Without wishing to underplay the Petrine dimension, nor intending any disrespect to St Peter, a distortion enters into Catholic identity if we reduce its whole living communal reality to the Petrine element alone.

For some, the Catholic problem appears more like an environmental threat, as though our identity is like that of a polar bear on a shrinking island of ice. It may be of little consolation if the animal knew that some of its kind survives quite well at *Sea World* down there on the Coast. There has indeed been a change in the Catholic environment. In the course of this past century, a huge demographic shift in the composition of the Catholic Church has occurred. At the beginning of the twentieth century, seventy per cent of Catholics were in Europe and North America. At its end, that percentage is found in the Southern regions of the world, namely in Africa, South America, Asia, Oceania. The Synod of Africa brought

---

2. <http://www.vatican.va/roman_curia/pontifical_councils/chrstuni/angl-comm-docs/rc_pc_chrstuni_doc_20050516_mary-grace-hope-christ_en.html>

this home to us. This is to say that most Catholics today belong to the younger, poorer, non-white (or racially mixed), politically unstable, and culturally religious parts of the planet, in contrast to the rich, secular, economically dominant, aging and secularised populations of North Atlantic countries. Of course, Australia is somehow in the middle of all this—not quite one or the other. But go to any of the bigger city parishes on Sunday and you will know what I mean. Our familiar Irish-Catholic world has so clearly changed.

On the other hand, the loss may be more particular and irritating, not so much a loss of identity, but a loss of particularly elusive something that needs to be there. Yes, it is a bit like that odd sock in the dryer. We certainly have one sock; and in terms of resources and organisation and professional expertise, it is a splendid sock. However, the other sock was somehow lost in the wash . . . the sock of vision, or faith, confidence, creativity and sense of purpose, it may be—the Catholicity from within, of faith, hope and love. As we backtrack through the washing and drying cycle of this past fifty years, how is it to be retrieved?

We all know that there are seasons for the freeze and the thaw that the polar bear can't do much about. We all know that losing the occasional sock is basic to the human condition of modern life. An identity loss, however, is rather more threatening than environmental or laundry problems. Questions nibble at the edges, and even start biting into the centre, of what was easily and assertively assumed in ages past to constitute 'catholic identity'.

Agathon: A Journal of Ethics and Value in the Modern World, Vol 9/2022

A Christian Vision and Today's Great Hospital

Anthony Kelly CSsR

Hospitals are not places where you stand back and wait for something to happen. Everyone is involved in a in a surge of activity, picked up and carried along, sometimes floating, sometimes submerged and struggling for air, all the time in a happening world, a stream of events interrupted with questions and under the pressure of problems. The weight of paperwork and the imposition of masks . . . But you move on, supported with a network of connections and bearing the weight of responsibilities for so many others: whispering in your every waking moment are insistent voices—of promises to keep in a common commitment to do the very best for the sick and suffering.

Every hospital is an embodiment of a hopeful vision. It shares a sense of our universal mortality and yet on many occasions it rightly celebrates the good effects of working together in the face of all familiar threats to health and well-being. A hospital is science and hope in action. It represents a remarkable ecology of healing in a complex whole of people and groups, staff and patients enter into field of healing activity so that each can act for the well-being of the human family.

Health professionals are familiar with the faces of suffering and death . . . and, in some final sense, each is faced with the limits of human existence. When the face of the sufferer turns to them in hope, they can ease pain, offer professional care, and, in the normal course of events, offer some hope of recovery from the isolation and apathy that sickness brings. But in the end, there are ancient limits, and all must face them. In the silence beneath all words there is an uncrossable frontier in everything, for all are exposed to the wonder and the fragility of our human condition. For the health professional there is a special a burden of looking into the face of suffering. Yes, there is hope, there is healing, and there is defeat, for a hospital is a laboratory of common humanity. We live, we die; and yet, even at that dark limit, Christian hope opens to life redeemed, restored, made whole in God.

What was once so clear and largely spontaneous has become infinitely complex. The brilliance of modern medicine, so splendidly instanced in the research programs and specialisations of a modern teaching hospital, has undreamt of resources compared to the past— and a lot of new problems. It has been wryly remarked that is present age is populated by the longest living hypochondriacs ever to burden the globe. The sobering point, however, is that even those medically assisted into increased longevity, often confess to surviving rather than living with a sense of meaning, in themselves, in their families, in their society, in their world.

What, in the light of Christian faith, can be said about health and healing today? It can contribute only a tiny aside to a huge conversation involving everything and everyone in the vigorous development of the living tradition of teaching and learning, of healing and helping that health professionals actually embody. There are so many questions. The blind person tapping his way through an unseen world through the deft use of a white cane is a great example. We are all in the dark in so many ways. We tap our way forward with the white stick of our prior experience, training, and overall sense of reality. As the white stick becomes a living extension of oneself, you hold it too loosely, it is just a foreign body, one more thing in the way. On the other hand, holding it too tightly is to be constricted to what we expect things to be as to be ill-prepared for sudden and surprising turns in the contours of the space in which we move. The path ahead lies open only by being true to what you have learnt while living that truth with flexibility and hope.

The Christian tradition of health care holds within itself the hope of eternal life infinitely surpassing this present form of life. In the meantime, 'life is fired at us point-blank' (Ortega y Gasset). Considering all the dynamics and structural levels implicit in what and who we are, no simple description seems possible. Nature and person, body and soul, psyche and spirit, man and woman, child and adult, individual and community, healthy and sick, innocent and guilty, society and culture, history and cosmos, universe and

God—these are just some of the dualities employed in our unfinished self-descriptions. As human beings we seem destined to make life complicated.

The languages available to our search for human meaning often foreshorten the possibilities of an answer. For example, most of us are at least politically aware of how racist or sexist language expressions preclude the recognition of equality in a democratic society. Communication is hampered by alienating dialects of prejudice and ignorance. The current revulsion against the flat, quantitative, purely economic description of society which is so favoured in modern politics, demands a more humane communication. Another source of alarm is the increasing robotisation of the human communication being reduced to such terms as stimulus and response, conditioning, input and output, turned on and switched off, being burned out or blowing fuses, doing one's thing, or being programmed or brain-washed, developing in cycles or stages, possessing 'magnetism', the right chemistry, or of projecting the right image, and so on . . . There is the obvious danger of linguistically replacing the total range of consciousness with the model of the machine, the computer, chemical or physical interaction, or the camera, the projector and the calculator. Language is formative. We speak a language; and it speaks us.

And yet the words of the poet, the cadences of great music, the silence of the mystic, the radiant witness of moral integrity communicate, with the holy scriptures of a great religious tradition, along with the stumbling, patient efforts of sufferers to name their pain, each in their different ways, express something more. Even though questions remain: if to be human is to be nourished and clothed and worded by a particular culture, what if the culture is distorted, stunted, wrong? A culture which sees only problems with no sense of a larger grace or mercy and hope, no longer able to acknowledge failure, fear, hurt, responsibility or hope, may find a fragile solace in blaming others or other times for its troubles. But that is just a step along the way to increasing depression. Perhaps in disgust, some will seek to transcend the world of problems by taking refuge in a form of mystical otherworldliness or narcotic dependency. Such ploys are of limited creative value. In the end, any culture that systematically represses the wholeness of experience, that prevents certain questions being raised, that reduces all values to personal gratification or control is inevitably on the way to becoming a slum or a kindergarten.

Such cultural distortions are what Christian tradition terms 'original sin'– that mutilated sense of self communicated by the culture in which one lives. 'Original sin is the socialised truncation of human life, the systematic reduction of each child of mystery to the banal world of man's own making.' The result is a terrifying loss of soul. A basic trauma is afflicting all cultures at every stage of world history.

The need for new models is being felt, in economics, politics, culture, and public health, in the exploration of reality itself. This impetus to reclaim something, once essential but now lost to our humanity, is being expressed in many ways. We seem to be under the necessity of becoming more intelligent about the limits that mere technical intelligence has imposed. In other words, the truth of Blaise Pascal's observation is being borne out: 'The heart has reasons which reason itself does not know'. A 'Second Enlightenment' more hospitable to needs of the human soul is called for. Human consciousness deserves more than experimental psychologist's models based on the laboratory rat, and the clinical psychologist's concerns limited to the diseased mind. It needs more than the economist's concern for a productive unit or the market's need for more consumers. What is needed is a larger vision open to the heights as well as depths in human consciousness. Body, soul and spirit must be given their due. Our whole humanity, scratching like a cat in a cupboard, wants to be let out. The distinctively human is demanding a larger vocabulary for its expression.

In the meantime, we human beings are complicated creatures. A hundred organs governed by so many interacting systems—neural, endocrinal, cardio-vascular, digestive, and so forth, with some two hundred bones, six hundred muscles, billions of cells and trillions of atoms somehow come together to makes each of us physically who we are. So much can go wrong! If we occasionally have a headache it is worth remembering that in that one and half kilos of finely wired organic matter in our heads there is more operational complexity than in the whole of the Andromeda Galaxy. In the trillion neurones of the human brain, each cell communicates with at least a thousand others. Scientists compute that the number of possible associations might exceed the number of atoms in the entire universe. Needless to say, we defer to their expertise. But it does suggest that we are not simple beings. Situate all this within the current environmental and ecological concerns of our day, and grave questions arise. Pollution of air, water and soil have their effects. The jury is still out on possible dangers of genetically modified crops, for an ecology developing over millions of years obviously deserves some respect. Anything as complicated as a planet inhabited by a millions and half species of plants and animals which have hitherto lived together in an equilibrium enabling them to use and re-use the same molecules of air and soil must not be rashly interfered with for some short term gain, especially if it results in a wholesale diminishment of the genetic stock. Public health today, therefore, necessarily involves environmental considerations, just as it implicitly confronts us with issues related to the ecological health of the planet itself.

And yet, here we are, in this moment of time, alive on this planet, immersed in this universe, just as both earth and universe are alive to themselves in us. Our bodies, minds and hearts are part of an awakening cosmic mystery. St Paul described the whole of creation as groaning in one great act of giving birth. He saw us human beings as groaning too, for the fulfilment that is not yet; more mysteriously, he understood the creative Spirit of God groaning within us to inspire hopes worthy of the mystery at work (Rom 8:18–28).

In other words, the sense of creation offered to us today brings together an appreciation of how we human beings are from God— 'children of God' in the biblical sense—and 'children of the universe, born of the earth. We are made in the image of God, and yet we are earthlings: we live only in a genetic solidarity with myriad other forms of life on this planet. If they serve and sustain us, we are called to a responsible stewardship of them. We human beings are related in a web of life with some millions of other species. Waratahs and wallabies, kookaburras and king prawns, frill-necked lizards and ferns—in the one web of life, they are all our relatives in a wondrous cosmic solidarity. Elements of the stars are in the phosphorous of our bones. The same hydrogen which makes the stars burn, energises our bodies and powers our imagination. We are the outcome of an amazing providence, that has brought us to this moment and given us the faith and hope and love, the courage and the intelligence we now possess.

At each moment, we are brought back to square one: what are we really and ultimately involved in? That is a disconcerting question since change is omnipresent. And because there are many worlds of problems and responsibilities, the prevailing mood of most institutions today is one of depression. Challenge is fine; some love it; but responsibility-overload is something else, especially when we all feel ourselves to be such bumbling amateurs in a world that won't let us simply get on with what we happen to know about. Still, a greater integrity in our sense of human wholeness is emerging, and it is one that is already deeply influential in present health-practise. Gone are the days when you could just think of the sufferer as a diseased individual body. Along with medical specialists, carers, and skilled administrators, there is the pastoral care team, the chaplain, the counsellor and the psychiatrist, the social worker—each standing for a larger context of connections and relationships and influences. How can we list all the levels of good that enter into the total human good? Aristotle's description of the human as *zoon logikon*, the "thinking animal" is a good place to start, but hardly the whole story. The peculiar complexity of the human phenomenon is inexhaustible: the organs, the bones, muscles, tissues, cells, molecules and atoms which somehow conspire to constitute our embodied selves are a phenomenon calling for an integrating sense of the whole. Scientific exploration has moved with exquisite sophistication into the very large and very small dimensions of reality. The quasar and the quark are more easily named than the human self. Science is more at home in the intergalactic than in the interpersonal. It is more familiar with sub-atomic indeterminacy than with human freedom or human well-being. Though chemistry and biology have dealt with the molecular and genetic structures of living things, they have paused, comparatively tongue-tied before the complexity of the human phenomenon. It has been easier for the scientist, as for us all, to avoid eye contact with another human being, or to ask what mystery has awoken in the consciousness we have of ourselves and others. It was perhaps safer to leave the human simply classified as one of the millions of species on this planet. But matters are beginning to change. One notable scientist, Heinz Pagels, considers the study of the complex human phenomenon 'the primary intellectual challenge to our civilisation for the next several centuries'.

We are complex beings, and in the acceptance of that, a vision of wholeness begins: however spiritual our aspirations, we cannot ignore the laws of physics, chemistry and molecular biology written into our emergence. Though faith concentrates on the ultimate self-transcendence of the human person in regard to God, it cannot disregard the activity of phenomena on prior levels, in the complex relationality of atoms, neurones and DNA molecules, cells, organs, organisms, bodies, bondings, populations, eco-systems, communities, societies, nations, global reality—all aspects of the body of our being together in this world.

In the current division of labour, pastoral care is expected to fly the flag of the big issues. A holistic health practice must be open to the ministrations of pastoral care—both its practitioners and the patients. A Christian vision of pastoral care implies an appreciation of human existence somewhat deeper than being a well-adjusted consumer in an economically rationalised society. But of course, as emerged from earliest Christian times, the care of the suffering is more than the 'care of souls'. Christian concern necessarily involves scientific medicine, professional competencies, economics, politics, and social concerns of the contemporary world. For Christian believers, the issue is the very notion of God, and what God is doing in the world. If believers pray that the Father's will be done and his kingdom come, pastoral care would seem to anticipate in some way what that will intends and in what the kingdom would be realised. Reflection on such utterly basic issues of faith and prayer necessarily lead into the Christian practice of pastoral care.

One of the most valuable aspects of the pastoral care tradition is its holistic sense both of the person and society. It is ministry and kind of care directed to the whole of life in all its predictable phases or dramatic turns. Death, for instance, is given its due, to be candidly recognised, accepted and approached through trust in him who is 'the resurrection and the life'. Evil is more than sickness, and guilt more than a depressive state. Pastoral care meets life in its heights and depths. Life typically goes through marriage, family and in the manifold relationships of a wider community composed of many generations. Since it is presupposed that the individual is a social being, a large part of care must be directed to the social well-being of the community. Though there may not have been much theory, pastoral care gave rise to schools, hospitals and charities of all kinds. Indeed, when one reviews even the fairly recent past it is hard to avoid the conviction that never was so much done by so many to such good effect—but with such little critical reflection! To that degree, a manifold holistic experience is sedimented in the tradition of pastoral care. It awaits a transposition into the present context which, while being rich with the promise of new possibilities, it awaits its proper multi-disciplinary elaboration and implementation as Church-sponsored organisations and institutions, feel the tension: an original expansive pastoral vision that gave rise to hospitals, schools and social services in all their variety, must now confront the requirements of professionalism, economic accountability, especially if governments were involved, and, of course, the constraints of the new style management.

A new urgency enters pastoral care and the many possibilities of its development within the larger collaborative context of Public Health as it turns to a variety of social problems. People are tempted to drive carelessly if they have just been sacked, or if their marriage has just broken down. Drugs provide some relief if prospects of getting a job have dwindled. Depression becomes endemic when there is every reason to be depressed. It is a long path from symptoms to the diagnosis of the disease –and then to see the disease as a possible symptom of a wider deeper breakdown of society. A collaborative public health sector at least provides a context in which deeper matters might be properly discussed. Any given society can suffer not only from physical disease, not only from psychological depression, but also from a 'pneuma-pathology', a debility of spirit, a culture-sickness. Faced with the problems of youth suicide and drug addiction, the prevalence of depression, and the isolation of the old in nursing homes, radical questions arise. When there is no language to articulate the deep things of life and death, both carers and their clients are enclosed in the same mute defeat.

Still, there is the flow of experience. Our senses place us in an environment. Our intelligence awakens to a field of forms and meaning. Our capacities to reflect and judge make us trustworthy mediators of the real world. Our feelings for the good, and our decisions in its regard, invite us into a collaborative world of moral value. For people of faith, the grace of God places them in a universe of ultimate meaning and worth. Instead of giving way to cynical disillusionment it rejoices in the whole truth, the love that faith inspires ‘bears all things, believes all things, hopes all things, endures all things. Love never ends . . ’ (1 Cor 13:4–8). It is the source of freedom and the refusal to be enslaved to the dispiriting forces of the situation.

Hospitals live in the midst of life and death, and suffering in all its forms. True, the world is not one vast hospital; but a great hospital, if it keeps its nerve and does not lost heart, can make the world a more hospitable place. It can be so the voice of sanity in the midst of madness, where the best of humanity and science and spirituality and faith fuse together in a unique blend in that community of men and women who are prepared to put a life into caring for sufferers in their elemental needs . . .

Contributors

Tony Brennan has been Director of Mission at Calvary Health Care Hobart for seven years. Prior to that worked for the Society of St Vincent de Paul for four years and in Catholic Education for twenty-five years. He has a Masters in Educational Leadership and a Masters of Theology.

Anthony Kelly CSsR, has taught systematic theology at Yarra Theological Union, been its president, president of Melbourne College of Divinity, Professor of Theology at Australian Catholic University (ACU), a member of the International Theological Commission, and a Fellow at ACU. Over his long and productive career he has produced over twenty-five books and booklets and countless book chapters and articles, from high level theological debates to popular spirituality.

Hilary Dominic Regan is publisher of ATF Press and systematic theologian. For many years worked as a Registered Nurse in health care institutions, public and private and as a 'volunteer' in service delivery in the Amazon, Brazil.

Timothy Radcliffe OP taught scriptures at Oxford and was elected provincial of English province of the Dominican Order in 1988. In 1992, he was elected master of the Dominican Order, holding that office until 2001. Author of over ten books and many articles in edited books and journals. In January 2023 Pope Francis named Radcliffe to lead a three-day preparatory retreat for participants in the synod on synodality in October 2023 which was held in Rome.

Gordon Watson taught systematic theology at Trinity Theological College, the Uniting Church's theological college in Brisbane, Queensland and held various positions in the Uniting Church in Victoria.

Printed in the USA
CPSIA information can be obtained
at www.ICGtesting.com
JSHW022234170324
59187JS00003B/239